THE BUCKINGHAMSHIRE VILLAGE BOOK

The places, the people and their stories

Buckinghamshire Federation of Women's Institutes

COUNTRYSIDE BOOKS
NEWBURY BERKSHIRE

First published 2020
© Buckinghamshire Federation of Women's Institutes

COUNTRYSIDE BOOKS
3 Catherine Road
Newbury, Berkshire

To view our complete range of books please visit us at
www.countrysidebooks.co.uk

ISBN 978 1 84674 394 8

All materials used in the manufacture of this book carry FSC certification.

Produced by The Letterworks Ltd., Reading
Designed and Typeset by KT Designs, St Helens
Printed by Holywell Press, Oxford

🍁 FOREWORD

This book is to celebrate the centenary of the Federation of Women's Institutes in Buckinghamshire, having been formed in 1920. I have lived in the county on and off since my childhood and I have taken great pleasure in collating and reading all the stories and photos that the WI members have sent to me for inclusion in this commemorative book.

'The Leafy County' is how many of us refer to Buckinghamshire colloquially and the numerous beech trees, amongst others, reflect the open country and natural features that attract people to visit the rolling countryside of the Chiltern Hills, Vale of Aylesbury and around the Great Ouse.

Much of the area has been classified as green belt and is popular with London commuters. However, mass urbanisation in the 20th century of the very north of the county saw the new town of Milton Keynes being formed.

Buckinghamshire is a ceremonial county in the South East of England, and the 16th-century farmhouse Chequers, near Ellesborough, is famous for being the country house of the incumbent Prime Minister.

Great Brickhill – 7 & 9 Heath Road

It has been an honour to have been involved with the making of this book and I feel sure that those who have not visited the villages of Buckinghamshire before will not hesitate to partake of their idiosyncrasies, beauty, history and possibly even meet some of the WI members who have contributed to the narrative! Thanks to all our inspiring WI members.

Pat Poole
Chairman, Buckinghamshire Federation of WIs

 ## ACKNOWLEDGEMENTS

The production of this book has only been possible by the enthusiastic research of the contributors and the untiring efforts of Pat Poole, who co-ordinated the project brilliantly.

A huge thank you to all who contributed – writers, artists and photographers. You have all played an important part in making this book a picture of life in Buckinghamshire in the 21st century.

County of BUCKINGHAMSHIRE

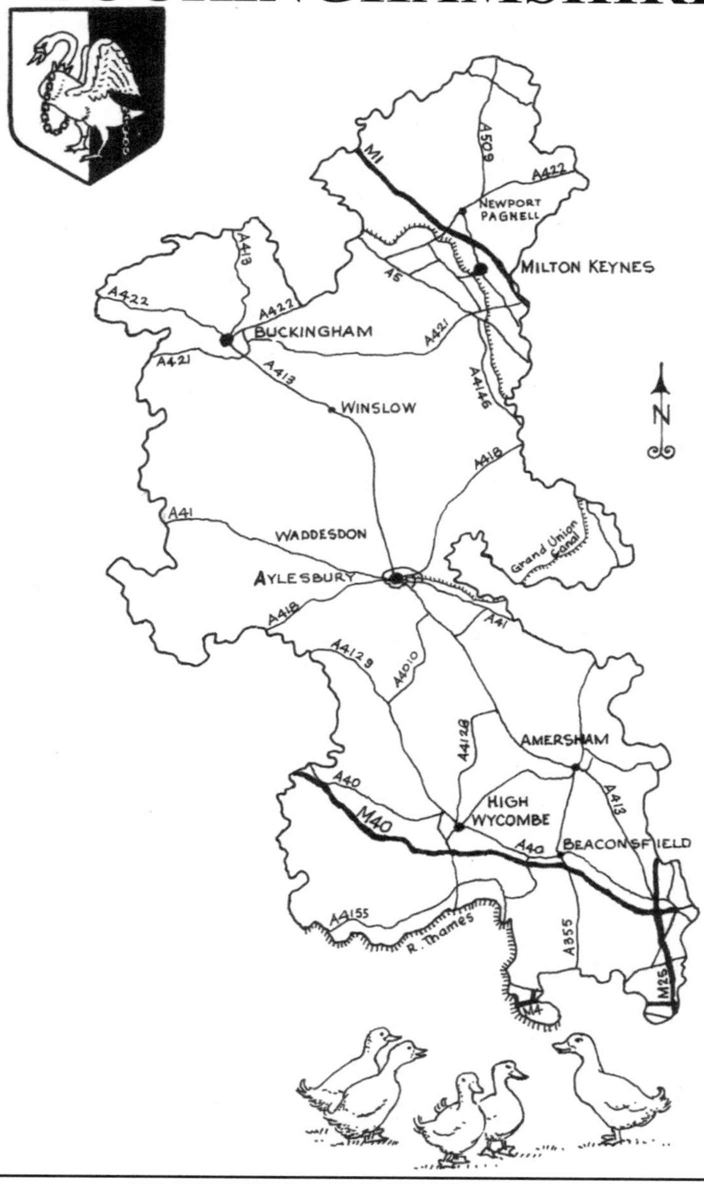
M1
A509
A422
NEWPORT PAGNELL
MILTON KEYNES
A413
A422
A422
A5
BUCKINGHAM
A421
A421
A413
A4146
WINSLOW
N
A418
A41
WADDESDON
Grand Union Canal
AYLESBURY
A418
A41
A4129
A4010
A4128
AMERSHAM
A40
HIGH WYCOMBE
M40
A413
A40
BEACONSFIELD
A4155
R. Thames
A355
M25
M4

🍁 ADSTOCK

Adstock is about half the size of its neighbour, Padbury, and is situated some 2 miles south, off the A413 to Aylesbury. Travellers along this road will miss it completely although it is only a hundred yards away. They are missing a treat. It is a delightful village and more compact than its neighbour. It also has a 13th-century church and a very attractive and popular pub. In Adstock, the old chapel has been turned into the village hall and the old school is now a private residence. Here too there are families of long standing as well as many newcomers.

Adstock – from 'Adda's stock' meaning 'Adda's field' began as a clearing in the Bernwood Forest. Like many Buckinghamshire villages it is mentioned in Domesday. Also like many of the county's ancient villages, it was virtually self-contained until the middle of the 20th century, with farms and local craftspeople supplying most of its needs. Still surrounded by farmland, it has lost its shop, post office and school. However, Adstock is still a thriving village with an active social life centred on the church, village hall and the Old Thatched Inn. It also has a children's playground and a village orchard where villagers gather in the autumn to make their own apple juice and cider and enjoy a day of associated activities.

The Adstock Singers perform in the local area at charitable events. There are Science and History Clubs which meet each month and many other social activities – book clubs, quizzes, suppers etc which are held in homes, the Village Hall and the pub. They have special events for children at Halloween and Christmas, plus carols around the tree in the centre of the village. Perhaps the highlight of the year for many is the Open Gardens Weekend when people from far and near come to admire our lovely, usually hidden, gardens. It truly is a delightful village to visit, or more especially to live in.

🍁 AMERSHAM

The history of the beautiful Market Town of Amersham goes back to Anglo-Saxon times, when it was known as Agmodesham, later becoming Elmodesham. By the time of the Domesday Book in 1086, it was referred to as Amersham. The land was mostly owned by Geoffrey de Mandeville, who obtained a charter from King John in 1213 for a Friday market and an annual fair on 19 September. Both these events continue to this day.

In 1521 seven Lollard dissenters were burned at the stake in Amersham. They died for their principles of religious liberty and for the right to read the Bible in English. The Lollard movement, which started in the mid-14th century, protested against the excesses of the Catholic Church. This was before the English Reformation took place, during which the Church of England broke away from the Pope and the Roman Catholic Church. There is a memorial to the dissenters, built in 1931, above the Old Town and the events have also been commemorated in a community play performed in St Mary's Church.

In the 19th century, Amersham became well-known for black lace, brewing, tanning and brick-making. During the Second World War, the Radiochemical Centre, a scientific research establishment, arrived in Amersham and this later became Amersham International. It is now known as GE Healthcare.

The Metropolitan Railway came to Amersham in 1892 and, as the local family – the Drakes of Shardeloes – did not want the railway on their land, the line was established at the top of the hill. In this way, Amersham-on-the-Hill became part of 'Metroland'.

In the 20th century, Old Amersham was home to two very contrasting businesses. At one end of the High Street was the Goya perfume factory, and at the other end was Brazils, who made sausages and pies. The pigs were apparently driven down Station Hill to meet their unknown fate!

Amersham has proven to be a very popular film location. Most famously, *Four Weddings and a Funeral* used The Kings Arms for external shots and a room at The Crown for other scenes. The famous modernist Grade II-listed house, built by Amyas Connell in 1929, known as High & Over has also been used as a film location. In 1973 it featured in a BBC documentary, made by John Betjeman, about Metroland.

The grave yard behind the church is the last resting place of Ruth Ellis, the last woman to be hanged in England. Ruth Ellis was hanged for murder in 1955 and her remains were moved to Amersham in the 1970s. She was buried under the name Ruth Hornby and tragically her son destroyed the gravestone shortly before his suicide in 1982.

Today Amersham is a thriving town, with a population of approximately 18,000. Many people commute to London for work, but enjoy the benefits of the beautiful countryside surrounding the town and the good local schools. Old Amersham is home to numerous shops and a variety of restaurants. There is an excellent museum which holds regular events and exhibitions on local history.

Amersham Angels WI is lucky to have its regular meetings in the historic Market Hall. This was built in 1682 and stands prominently on stone stilts in the High Street. For over 300 years it has been used for meetings of importance, including the first meeting of the Amersham Parish Council in 1895 and as a recruiting base for the First World War in 1914. Of special note are the stone buffers, built against the pillars so there would be no corners for 'vagrants' to sleep in! These were not compassionate times. Another notable building, with a sad past is the workhouse in Whieldon Street built by Sir Gilbert Scott in 1838. It later became Amersham Hospital and subsequently has been converted into flats.

It is no surprise, however, that these days Amersham regularly features in lists of the best places to live. This picturesque market town, surrounded by the Chiltern Hills, combines the very best of old and new, within a thriving community.

❧ ASHENDON

Ashendon, including Upper and Lower Pollicott, is a small village which has two entries in the Domesday Book and still retains its designation as a Saxon Hundred. It is set in a conservation Area of Outstanding Natural Beauty, with panoramic views over Aylesbury Vale.

Ashendon has changed considerably in the last 30 years, no longer being an entirely agricultural community. It has gradually absorbed urban commuters and their young families, although about 25 houses are still occupied by residents with connections to the old farming families. There are now 110 houses or cottages in the village, with a population of approximately 270.

The three remaining farming families make use of modern machinery, requiring fewer farm workers. With the mainline railway station only 6 miles away, providing a good service into London, and the A41 and M40 within easy reach, many residents do not work locally – unless it is from home. There is no village school in Ashendon, so the village children also commute and all shopping has to be brought in.

The 12th-century church of St Mary's sits on top of the hill, as it has for over 800 years. Many of the villagers help maintain this Grade I listed building, as well as attending services, as part of the Bernwode Benefice. The Benefice is made up of 7 parish churches, including Ashendon. The old pub, originally named The Red Lion, was used as a court house in the past, and has been rechristened a number of times. It is now known as The Hundred of Ashendon. It serves as a centre for village activities, as well as providing accommodation and restaurant facilities. The 'Sloe Nouveau' and Christmas auction evenings, run by the Red Lion Social Club, attract many villagers and the latter raises funds for both the church and village community. The Red Lion Social Club also provides an annual meal at the pub for villagers over pensionable age. The annual Gatehangers dinner for the men of the village still takes place, as it has done since 1962, when 'The Gate' is awarded to the man who has contributed the most to the village over the year. The Ashendon WI was founded in 1939.

The Ashendon Playing Fields Association manages the village playing field and pavilion, and raises funds to maintain the football pitch, children's playground and outdoor Multi Use Games Area, all of which provide excellent amenities for sports tournaments and local fetes. The old village school, which was converted into the village hall in 1952, is a small but well-equipped venue for village activities. The annual harvest supper and church bazaar take place there, as well as regular film shows, private parties and meetings of various village associations.

Ashendon is a very welcoming village and a delightful place to live. The community spirit pulls everyone together and manifests itself in many different ways; from raising over £35,000 in three weeks to ensure that fast fibre broadband cables were brought to the village, to the annual progressive supper, when villagers move between each other's houses, partaking of a different course in a different house and finishing at the pub – where the conviviality continues!

❧ ASHLEY GREEN

Ashley Green is a village and civil parish, close to the boundary with Hertfordshire and midway between Chesham and Berkhamsted.

It is one of the villages in Buckinghamshire which still retains a village charm in spite of the pressures of the 21st century. With a village hall, old school, church and pub at the centre of village life, Ashley Green feels like a place where you would want to live.

There are many local residents who have lived and raised children here, whose families continue to live in the village, along with several farms surrounding the area. With the London Underground and mainline railway stations nearby, and easy access to the A41, M25 and M1, it is a popular home for commuters who travel daily into London.

Originally a hamlet within Chesham parish, its name derives from the Old English for Ash Field, referring to the forest that once covered this part of the Chiltern Hills.

Land for an Anglican church was provided by Lord Chesham, and St John's Church was built and endowed by the gift of Elizabeth Dorrien of Clifton, Bristol, in memory of her sisters. Ashley Green became a separate ecclesiastical parish in 1876 and is now part of the Greater Chesham group of churches. In 2010, a kitchen and toilet was installed in the church and a time capsule, including a newspaper and a photograph of the congregation, was buried under the floor of the kitchen.

Ashley Green has one public house, The Golden Eagle, referred to locally as 'The Eagle'. The first official reference to an ale house in the village is dated 1692, when the landowners, farmers and residents debated, gossiped and quenched their thirst at 'the house on the path near the village green'.

By the time of Queen Victoria, the well-farmed land around the village enjoyed prosperity thanks to the patronage of the royal household – which owned orchards in the village. A licence was granted to a cottage tenant to use the property to 'sell intoxicating liquor'. Thus, in 1856, Samuel Blake opened his door as a public house called 'The Eagle'.

On the junction of Chesham Road and Hog Lane, the corner house used to be a shop and post office. An old post box still remains, built into one of the entrance posts. There is also a farm shop at Johns Lane Farm, selling all manner of local produce.

The Ashley Green Village School was attended by all the local children and was the subject of a documentary film (*Village School*, 1940) directed by John Eldridge. This film starred Mrs James, the headmistress of the school, and Mrs Glover, the other teacher at the school. Many of the pupils are shown taking part in school activities, both indoors and outdoors. Some of these pupils were evacuees. The film was a tribute to Britain's female teachers in wartime and was used to show America that life went on regardless during the war, with the hope of encouraging them to join the war effort. There is also a more recent documentary, which includes one of the boys in that film – now a local man in his 80s – being interviewed to explain what life was like in 1940.

Around 1982, the village school closed and Lord Chesham gifted the site, and the buildings on it, to the village. There was the old school itself, with one wing known as the bungalow – the home of the headmistress and family, a 1950s building which was used as the kitchen for school meals, and the reading room. The latter – looking like a little tin church – was erected after the First World War for the men of the village to come and read the papers.

After its closure, a group was set up to deal with the maintenance of the old school and to manage lettings to anyone who wanted to hire it, with an emphasis on community events. There was already a village hall – known as the Memorial Hall – on the green. The two groups merged, and the Ashley Green and District Community was formed to run both sites and to stage events for the community. Such events include the annual Village Fair on the green, the annual Bonfire Night, a Burns Night supper, quiz nights and many other well-attended events. The Queen's Jubilee celebrations and royal weddings have also been screened there, for the community to come and watch together.

The buildings are also used by other groups for such activities as Pilates and Zumba, several playgroups, art classes, bridge club, ballet and many others too numerous to list here. Behind the village hall, in The Glebe, there is a small play area and some allotments. There is also a well on the green outside the entrance gates to the old school.

Finally, there is an Ashley Green Women's Institute. This is a thriving group with many interesting speakers throughout the year, coffee afternoons in gardens, and lunches in the pubs and restaurants in the area. It is very popular and attracts ladies from the surrounding towns and villages, often outnumbering the villagers themselves!

🍁 ASTON CLINTON

Aston Clinton started out as a small hamlet and is thought to date from Saxon times. It was known as 'Estone' in the Domesday Book, but by the 13th century was known as Aston or Eston. The family name of William de Clinton was added in the 14th century as Edward III gave the manor to his good friend. Today its residents are fighting hard to keep Aston Clinton a village and not a suburb of Aylesbury. Aston Clinton used to have the A41 going through the centre of the village, but a by-pass built in 2003 has given developers the opportunity to build on the countryside within the village.

Many roads in Aston Clinton, both new and not so new, reflect the history and people who have lived here. Aston Clinton is well known as a Rothschild village – the village hall is named after Sir Anthony Rothschild – and the old school, West Lodge hotel and many other buildings are testament to the family's connection with the village. There were, however, other benefactors who helped the community of Aston Clinton and who have streets named after them.

In Margaret Lowe Place, just off London Road, the houses stand where Miss Lowe's house originally stood. Born in 1915 to teacher parents, she lived all her life in Aston Clinton, was a teacher herself and became a governor of the local school. She was 90 when she died, and had served 30 years as a Parish Councillor, 19 years on Aylesbury Vale District Council and was involved in many other local organisations, including the football club. Most of all, she will be remembered by Buckland, Drayton Beauchamp and Aston Clinton WI as being one of its members for 20 years.

Gordon Smith Close is named after Gordon Smith, who was a road sweeper in the village for some years. He died in 2013 and was laid to rest in the village graveyard. In 2015, the Parish Council agreed that it was a fitting tribute to name a new road after the local resident 'who had dedicated his life to cleaning up the village'. He is also remembered by a stone plaque of his head on the wall of the café in the park. He looks a very jolly man, and proves that you don't have to be of the nobility or famous to make an impact where you live.

☘ AYLESBURY

Nestled in the middle of Buckinghamshire's County Town of Aylesbury is the Old Town – a village within the town. The Old Town is a conservation area, whose boundary is the inner ring road and at whose centre sits St Mary's Church and Square. Visitors are often surprised to discover this small and intimate village centre, with its historic 16th- and 17th-century houses, interesting buildings and sense of community.

As well as St Mary's Church, other denominations include the Methodist Church, Evangelical Church and one of the earliest Quaker

Meeting Houses. Prebendal House – once the home of John Wilkes, as well as the Liberty of London family – was a private school but is now divided into luxury flats, hidden behind the imposing wooden gates. The 15th-century Prebendal tithe barn, one of the oldest buildings in the town, is now a builder's yard.

The County Museum, originally the town's grammar school, displays local historical artefacts, arranges special art exhibitions, is home to the National Embroiderers' Guild collection and a Roald Dahl hands-on gallery, as well as providing a venue for the local Archaeological Society. There is also a secluded café within its walled garden.

The only pub, The King's Head, is owned by the National Trust and is a 16th-century coaching inn with an attractive cobbled courtyard where there are tables and benches. Oliver Cromwell is rumoured to have stayed here – although this rumour has since been proven to be untrue.

The turnover of residents is relatively low, adding to the village feel – along with a range of community activities such as celebrations for the Queen's Jubilee, the Big Lunch, an annual churchyard clean-up and the Secret Gardens of Old Aylesbury event attended by up to 700 friends and family of locals and organised by the Old Town Residents' Association. A welcome letter is delivered to newcomers to the Old Town, and residents are always happy to provide recommendations for local businesses and tradesmen.

Although the 'village' has no school, families are attracted by the many free events arranged by the Town Council. Highlights for the year include the WhizzFizzFest event, involving many local school children featuring characters from Roald Dahl's stories; the St George's Day Parade and the Charter Day. The Town Council are also responsible for the colourful, floral displays that can be seen in hanging baskets, on roundabouts and in troughs along the approaches into town.

The 'village' is within walking distance of many amenities – markets, shops, supermarkets, a theatre, a cinema, a leisure centre, a train station and a range of cafés and restaurants. The Chiltern Hills are on the doorstep, just a short bus or train ride away. For those who enjoy chamber music, there is a lunchtime concert every Thursday in St Mary's Church, except during August and at Christmas time. It is well worth a visit and it is free for under-18s. Occasional jazz and evening concerts are also held in St Mary's, along with organ recitals in the Methodist Church.

The churchyard and secret gardens provide a haven for wildlife, including red kites, swifts in the summer, tits of all types, gold crests, greenfinches, squirrels and bats. Peregrine falcons also nest on County Hall, although this is not strictly in the village.

Aylesbury Town WI is relatively 'young', at less than ten years old, but it is thriving with over 40 members of differing ages. Not all WI members live in the village, but a large number do and for those who come from elsewhere there are buses that come into the centre. Close by is a Women's Refuge, which is supported with donations of toiletries and clothes from the WI members. The lunch club is truly spoiled for choice and the craft and book group regularly meet in an ice cream parlour!

🍁 BALLINGER

This charming Buckinghamshire hamlet, and its common, is a peaceful place with a playground, cricket pitch and pavilion at its centre – where Ballinger Waggoners (young and not so young) have played for 60 years. High on the Chiltern ridge, and feeling quite remote, it is only a few miles from the end of the Metropolitan tube line and yet is as rural as you can get.

Much of the village was 'manorial waste' – not belonging to any Parish – following the Dissolution of the Monasteries by Henry VIII, before which it was probably part of the land associated with Missenden Abbey. It remained such until 1885 when it was taken over under the enclosure awards. Parts of the village still remains in uncertain ownership today.

Ballinger is in the heart of what used to be mainly cherry orchards, when agriculture provided the main income of the village. In times past, it was known as a paraffin village, having no electricity or mains drainage until 1990. People still remember the lavender lorry that once provided welcome relief to households with cesspits.

On the edge of the cricket field is Ballinger War Memorial Hall, built in the Arts and Crafts style to commemorate those who lost their lives in the First World War. This is now the centre of village activities, which include plays and pantomimes, meetings, parties and wedding receptions, exercise classes, the WI, the Arts Society and much more. BATS, the Ballinger Baby and Toddler Group, is run by volunteers and is treasured by the community as a Tuesday morning 'must' for all villagers aged between 0 and 4 – and their parents.

In days past, the village was a centre for straw-plaiting – providing the women of the village with their main occupation. One such was Rose Pearce, of Rose Cottage (naturally). From the hook in the middle of her sitting room, which is still in situ today, a chuddle pot full of liquid was placed for the straw to be soaked. A number of ladies would gather in the cottage to plait the straw and, after making and drying various baskets and other products, they would take them to the market in Tring to be sold. A good income was made from these, along with Rose's famous cherry pies.

In Blackfield Lane, the site of the original village pond a forge can be found. The forge still contains farriers' tools and artefacts.

Ballinger Memorial Hall

Nowadays, with easy rail access to London from Great Missenden and Chesham, many inhabitants commute for work, returning home to this beautiful, peaceful spot.

A story is told of the early days of the Second World War, when the Prime Minister, Winston Churchill, visited as the first bombs were dropped on the village by enemy planes – probably aiming for the Prime Minister's official residence, Chequers, in a nearby valley. The bombs injured some cattle, who lived with shrapnel in them to the end of their lives. Luckily, although frightened, none of the villagers were hurt.

At the end of Blackthorne Lane is the delightful tiny church of St Mary's, built in a garden in 1873 of brick and flint with whitewashed walls inside. Once a school and a lecture room for the poor, it became a mission hall with services alternating between the Free Church and the Anglican Church. It is now an Anglican church, part of the parish of St Peter and St Paul, Great Missenden. It aims to be a place of peace for those of faith and none, 'open to all as a tranquil place to rest with their thoughts.'

 BEACONSFIELD

Come high days and holidays, the resonant voice of Beaconsfield's Town Crier, Dick Smith, has signalled the start of Beaconsfield's celebrations and acts of remembrance since 1969. He is also master of its oral history and shares it with relish, telling tales of highwaymen who once lay in wait for the wealthy carriages en route along the busy road between London and Oxford, of the munitions factory set up in 1915 to feed the hungry guns of the First World War, of GK Chesterton holding court at the White Hart, and of a schoolboy called Terry Pratchett who fell in love with books at the town library.

Born and raised in this tightly knit market town community, Dick now serves a thriving commuter town with an ever-quickening pace of life. Within easy reach of London and Heathrow, and with excellent transport links, Beaconsfield is a visibly prosperous community, a very attractive place to live and bring up families, with good schools and GP surgeries, a lively library and two busy high streets of shops, cafés and restaurants. Beaconsfield also boasts world-famous Bekonscot, the world's oldest original model village, which opened to the public in 1929 and continues to delight everyone with its quirky village scenes, clacketing trains and brilliant shop name puns.

Beaconsfield is surrounded by a green belt of fields and woodland, and many of its roads are lined with trees to green the town. Tipping out of a crowded train from London Marylebone, it remains a pleasure to take a breath of fresh air, watch the red kites circle above and feel the city stress fall away.

Unsurprisingly then, demand to live here is high and house prices even higher. New homes are springing up everywhere, with blocks of flats and multi-million pound mansions replacing older, more modest homes. To the east, on land once owned by the Army, a large new development of over 300 houses is in progress, and far greater expansion is on the horizon. It is a time of growth and change. But this is nothing new.

Only the Old Town remains much as it might have looked in the 18th century. The timber frames of inns that crowded the main roads are still there, hidden behind brick facades, along with the fine houses that were built for gentry drawn from London by the clean air and pleasant landscape. The land itself was in the hands of wealthy landowners and it was they who profited from the rapid expansion of the town after the railway came in 1906, gradually selling off land around the station in parcels to accommodate the new commuters. This resulted in a town with not one but two centres, with a further community expanding in Holtspur to the west after the Second World War. One great estate, Hall Barn, remains a powerful force in the town, while road names and converted farmhouses serve as reminders of the town's agricultural past. It is still possible to walk out into beautiful countryside with ease, across fields that have been farmed for hundreds of years and in autumn through beech woods of copper and gold.

A small army of volunteers work hard to counter these effects and nurture the community. Thanks to their energy, there is something going on any day of the week. There are film shows at the world-renowned National Film and Television School – where Wallace and Gromit first took shape in the imagination of student Nick Park, concerts in churches, plays and musicals in community centres, and lunch clubs and tea parties for older residents. The young have the Brownies and Guides, Cubs and Scouts, Police and Air Cadets. There are WI evenings and U3A lectures, or public meetings to debate the future of the green belt; campaigns for cycle routes and against plastic usage; fundraising for charity; litter picking with the Scouts; tree and bulb planting to brighten the town, and a messy church for children.

Beaconsfield's calendar is bookmarked by public gatherings,

beginning with the traditional Charter Fair in May, which goes back (with interruptions) to 1296. There is the *Beaconsfield Now!* Family Day, Shakespeare in the open in the grounds of Hall Barn in June, a charity Country Fayre in August, the annual Service of Commemoration in November and a Festival of Lights in December. Each event draws the residents together, pulling them away from screens and sofas – making a community, not just a commuter town.

🍁 BELLINGDON

Bellingdon is a small village about a mile out of Chesham on a ridge of the Chiltern Hills, 600 feet above sea level.

Before the Second World War this was a close-knit community with most of the villagers employed in farming and brick-making. The squire was Mr William Lowndes who lived at The Bury in Chesham.

The annual fete was held in the squire's grounds and it was greatly looked forward to as there were so few amusements in those days.

The children walked to the next village at Asheridge to attend school. There were no buses and they walked through the fields and looked for the first honeysuckle leaves in the spring and they knew where the birds' nests were.

The church is still the centre of the village activities. It is a small wooden building about 120 years old. There is also a village hall which is a popular meeting place. Bellingdon villagers are keen gardeners and the annual horticultural show has an extremely high standard. The Hall is bursting at the seams when this is held as besides the wonderful displays of vegetables and flowers there are competitions for preserves and cakes, sewing and knitting and entries for the children's miniature gardens and animals made from vegetables.

🍁 BLEDLOW

> *'They who live and do abide*
> *Shall see Bledlow Church fall into The Lyde.'*

The Lyde, mentioned in this ancient local proverb, is a dell from which about nine springs issue forth, wearing away the soft chalk down to the harder greensand below and coming together to form a pond. This pretty dell in Bledlow remained until Dutch elm disease destroyed its elms in the 1970s. When efforts to save the elms proved futile, Lord and Lady Carrington embarked upon the creation of 'The Lyde Garden', a water garden containing interesting flora and features for the enjoyment of villagers and visitors. The Lord and Lady often gardened there, and their calls to their two wire-haired dachshunds would echo around the dell.

Standing in The Lyde Garden, it is possible to look up towards Holy Trinity Church, dating from the 12th century. The church is perched on a high mound above the waters of The Lyde, hence the ancient proverb. Why was the church built in what seems such a precarious spot? The probable explanation is that it was built on the site of an earlier, most likely wooden, church which was itself superimposed on a pre-Christian site where Pagan water-worship took place.

Bledlow village lies beneath Bledlow Hill, and between the two runs the ancient Upper Icknield Way which has prehistoric origins as a trade route between East Anglia and the south west of the country. Bledlow would have been an attractive resting place for travellers to water their animals and two tracks descend from the Upper Icknield Way to the village; one coming down from the old Leather Bottle (once a drovers' inn) and the other descending from The Cop, which was the site of an ancient tumulus of Bronze Age origin.

In early 11th-century records, Bledlow was called Bleddanhloew. '*Bledda*' was an Old English person's name and '*hlaw*' was a hill or barrow. Bledlow was a Saxon village, on the frontier between the West Saxon kingdom and the Danelaw. In the frequent skirmishes that occurred, the legend arose that a Saxon chieftan was slain and buried on The Cop.

At least one ghostly story applies to Bledlow. It is said that a nun from medieval times haunts the Lyde Path, which runs from the church to the bottom of the village. Inhabitants recall that until quite recently some villagers refused to walk down the path at night.

Through the middle of Bledlow runs the old Great Western Railway line, from Princes Risborough to Watlington, which took watercress and farm produce up to London. This fell into disuse in recent years, but has now been resurrected by Chinnor and Princes Risborough Railway Association as a restoration line. Ramblers walking through the fields in summer can enjoy the sight of a restored steam or diesel engine, and its carriages, charging along through the countryside. Those who attend Bledfest, a little rock festival held in September at Bledlow's lively cricket club, have sometimes enjoyed the spectacle of a steam engine's dramatic fiery entry at night as it halts, clouded in steam, alongside the club amid the music and festivities. Another branch of the railway, which ran to Thame, has been transformed into The Phoenix Trail for walkers, cyclists and horses to exercise free from motor traffic.

The old village workhouse, which for a time was a children's home before it became derelict, has passed into the hands of a private developer and is being restored for private accommodation. There is no longer a shop, a post office or a school in Bledlow, although a flourishing pre-school in the village hall attracts families with young children. Whilst the life of the village once depended mainly upon agriculture and small industries, such as the Paper Mill, the Smithy, and cottage lacemaking, the current inhabitants of Bledlow come from a wide variety of occupations. Farming is still very important, although farm workers are rarely seen outside their vehicles now. The proximity of the Chiltern Line, from Princes Risborough into Marylebone, allows people who live in Bledlow to work in London.

Murray's Buckinghamshire Guide, edited by John Betjeman and John Piper, described Bledlow Church in 1947 as follows: 'The large and stately interior is mercifully not electrified.' One cannot help speculating what they would say about the church today. Wall paintings carefully restored by English Heritage are now discernible thanks to electric lights, and a small kitchen and washroom have arrived.

Whilst the occupants of the village may now communicate over the internet more than the garden fence, there is good community spirit and a range of clubs and social groups who welcome new and long term inhabitants. On the same evening that WI members meet, their husbands and other village gentlemen attend a meeting of FAB – Fellows at Bledlow – to talk and eat in company. There is a very active cricket club with junior and senior teams; a social club known as The Bledlow Belles; a church choir, which not only sings in the church but performs in cathedrals up and down the country; an annual flower and produce show and a range of activities in the village hall. There is little occasion to be lonely or bored in this village.

❦ BLEDLOW RIDGE

The village of Bledlow Ridge sits perched happily in the Chiltern Hills. The name, meaning 'Bloody Hill', is said to commemorate a fierce battle between the Danes and the Saxons. It is part of the civil parish of Bledlow-cum-Saunderton and was originally part of the ancient ecclesiastical parish of Bledlow, which is mentioned in the Domesday Book. However, Bledlow Ridge gained separate status when St Paul's Church was built here in 1868.

St Paul's sits at the heart of the village. The beautiful stained-glass west window was designed by John Piper, one of Britain's leading artists. It has been described by author June Osborne as 'a rhapsody in many shades of blue … a window of great loveliness, and its subject, if it may be said to have one, is Heaven'.

The village is a popular place to live as it combines picturesque countryside with good transport links. There are direct trains to London Marylebone from Princes Risborough and Saunderton, and the M40 is only 5 miles away.

Today most of the village population are middle-aged adults and it has a higher number of retired people compared to the national average. However, with the under-20s making up just over 20% of the population the village still manages to maintain quite a youthful feel. The inhabitants of Bledlow Ridge today are mainly employed in managerial, administrative or professional roles. This contrasts sharply with times past when farming and more rural occupations would have been more common, such as lacemaking and the rather strangely named 'bodging' (the skilled craft of chair making). Even a few decades ago most people worked locally and there were more small businesses and light industry in the area.

There is a village shop, a highly rated primary school, a village hall and a thriving community-owned country pub, The Boot. The villagers bought the pub in 2010, saving it from being turned into a house.

Most of the properties in the village are relatively modern detached houses built following the Second World War. Prior to this, the area was very rural in character with scattered clusters of houses along the ridge. There are still some very old properties in the village, such as The Old Vicarage and Loxborough House, which provide a reminder of the history of the village. A story is told that Cromwell stabled his horse in barns next to Pankridge Farm, and the ghost of John Kingham, murdered in 1893, is said to walk the village at night and haunt Studmore Farm. An area of the village named 'The City' is thought to originate from refugees fleeing to the area from the City of London during the Great Plague of 1665. An old windmill used to be a prominent landmark until 1933, when Wycombe Rural District Council demolished it. Milling had stopped in 1914 after one of the main timbers broke.

The village has an active community and there are several clubs including the Cricket and Tennis Clubs, the Friendship Club, the Horticultural Society and the WI. The latter gained a place in history for its phenomenal jam-making record during the Second World War. There are annual charity events, including the Bonfire & Fireworks and the Ridge Off Roader race, as well as a host of one-off gatherings – bingo, lunches, suppers, coffee mornings and wine tastings – throughout the year.

The village has had quite a few notable residents over the years. Stewart Copeland, founder and drummer with the band The Police, lived at The Old House. Opera singer Betty Bannerman lived at Pankridge Farm and hosted small concerts in a converted barn there. The actor Leslie Phillips (best known for his catchphrase 'Ding Dong') owned Retreat Cottage for 40 years. Dr Paul Hawkins, who created the Hawk-Eye tracking technology used at Wimbledon and football matches, was originally from the village.

In truth, Bledlow Ridge offers a great welcome to visitors. The Yoesden Nature Reserve is on the doorstep and is considered by many as one of the jewels of the Chilterns AONB, with its traditional Chiltern landscape of chalk grassland with rare butterflies and wild flowers topped by hanger woodland. The area is home to red kites, great spotted woodpeckers, buzzards and rare butterflies, such as the Adonis Blue, and is decorated with lovely wild flowers like the Chiltern Gentian.

The glorious countryside around Bledlow Ridge and its surrounds attracts many walkers and cyclists. The Chiltern Way passes through the village and the Ridgeway, the ancient Icknield Way and the Phoenix Trail are also nearby. Most definitely worth a visit.

🍁 BOVINGDON GREEN

Bovingdon Green has a gentle village atmosphere and most of the people who live on the Green find that there is a friendly way of life. This friendship is helped by the fact that in 1968 a group of residents decided to form the Bovingdon Green Preservation Society. This society not only keeps the grass cut and the green looking tidy, but also has social and fund raising activities.

The village hall, built in 1926, is thriving at the present time, being used regularly by many groups including table tennis club, yoga classes, dog training and Parish Council Arts & Crafts.

🍁 BOW BRICKHILL

'Little Brickhill, Great Brickhill,
Brickhill with a Bow,
These three Brickhills
Stand all in a row.'

This linear village, clustered around the road to Woburn Sands and the steep hill up to a church, is situated in North Buckinghamshire just outside Milton Keynes. There are three Brickhill parishes – Bow Brickhill lies at the foot of the Bedfordshire Greensand Ridge, and Great Brickhill and Little Brickhill are elevated on the ridge itself.

The name Brickhill has its origins in 11th-century spellings of the word for hilltop. 'Brichelle' is the Norman spelling of 'bryk' and 'hylle', both British words; and Bow may originate from a family called Boel, who lived in the area in the 12th century, creating 'Bolle Brichulle' or 'Belle Brickhulle'.

Close by lies the site of a Roman settlement, Magiovinium, located across the fields of the Ouzel river valley.

Family names associated with the manor of Bow Brickhill are recorded from as far back as the 11th century: Gifford, Chauncey, Cheval, Woodville, Watson, Stanton and DeLap. The manor now belongs to the Duke of Bedford. Some names have been incorporated into districts of Milton Keynes, imaginatively linking past and present.

The Parish Church of All Saints holds a prominent position at the top of the hill and records indicate that the Chauncey family was involved in its establishment. It is built of rubble and local stone dressings, with a tile roof. Some parts date from the 12th century, with rebuilding in the 15th and 18th century when a noted local antiquarian Browne-Willis restored it after a long period of disuse. Recent restoration was completed in 2014. The tower has four bells dating from the mid-1600s. Due to its elevated position on the Greensand Ridge, it was used as a lookout in the Napoleonic War and by the Royal Observer Corps in the Second World War.

Bow Brickhill has a railway station, located a half-mile from the centre of the village. It was opened in 1905 on the Oxford to Cambridge Varsity line, of which only the Bletchley to Bedford branch still remains in operation. The line has been at risk of closure in the past, but the requirements of the London Brick Company in Stewartby and the development of Milton Keynes has helped to secure it. There are plans to re-instate the East West Rail route in the future and also to construct a parallel Oxford to Cambridge expressway road.

Climbing the hill to the woods gives access to the Greensand Ridge Walk, a long-distance footpath covering a 40 mile walk from Leighton Buzzard to Gamlingay. The woodland paths, from the church through beech and conifer woods, are popular with walkers, runners and cyclists. Paths also run alongside the Woburn golf courses.

There were originally two pubs, The Wheatsheaf on the main road – first constructed in 1600 as a half-timbered and thatch building – and The Plough at the bottom of Church Road. Only The Wheatsheaf continues as a thriving local restaurant. There are no longer any shops or a post office, but the school remains.

Farming was a major occupation in the past, with women and girls supplementing the family income with straw-plaiting and lace-making, and the men and boys felling timber for railway sleepers and pit props. There were six farms, Manor Farm, London End Farm, Rectory Farm, Tilbrook Farm, Battams Farm and Poplar Farm, with much of the land owned by the DeLap family. In the early days there was no mains water, so water had to be carried to homes and to livestock from local springs. Residents now commute to jobs in Milton Keynes, other surrounding towns and to London.

In 1916, children were given time off school and paid 1d per pound of blackberries picked around the village, which were then delivered by the headmaster to the collecting centre in Bletchley to make jam. Their medicinal quality was considered essential to the army provisions. Fundraising for a war memorial started in 1917, with dances and whist drives, and continued until its unveiling in March 1919.

In the 1920s, the Westminster Cathedral organist Dr Sydney Nicholson lived in the village and organised summer camps for the boys from the choir, who supplemented the singers in the church over the summer services.

A painting of Bow Brickhill, called 'A Village Choir' by Thomas Webster RA (1847), was given to the Victoria and Albert Museum in 1857. Bow Brickhill parishioners were the sitters for the singers and instrumentalists assembled in the west gallery of the church.

Bow Brickhill has a thriving village community, with many activities and local support groups being organised by volunteers for the benefit of residents. The development and growth of nearby Milton Keynes has changed the dynamics of the village, and residents are aware of the possibility of further change as Milton Keynes continues to expand. However, Bow Brickhill is classified as an Area of Attractive Landscape, and is appreciated and enjoyed by everyone in the area.

🍁 BRADWELL

Bradwell is one of 13 ancient villages in North West Buckinghamshire that now constitute Milton Keynes. It is situated on the road that runs north from Bletchley to Loughton, and on to Wolverton (home to the Royal Train) and Stony Stratford, linking to Watling Street.

The village has a recorded history dating back to the 11th century, as well as Roman ruins.

There are remains of an 11th-century Benedictine Abbey and Monastery.

The area was agricultural and, small as the village was, it had three separate farms. One of the farms is now a very busy youth hostel, and another a museum. There were stocks in the village, located beneath a large tree outside The Bell pub, thought to have been used up until the 18th century.

The building of the M1 in the 1950s brought considerable change to the rural life of North Buckinghamshire and the conglomerate of villages that became Milton Keynes. This did not meet with the local residents' approval and there was considerable protest. Bradwell had, by then, become known locally as 'Old Brad II' to disassociate it from New Bradwell, which had been developed in the 1850s with the growth of the railway works at Wolverton.

Milton Keynes brought extensive building of homes, schools and colleges, hospitals and clinics – NHS and private – and a glass and chrome shopping centre of a revolutionary design for the time, and Bradwell village escaped none of this upheaval.

All three farms ceased to be, but a farm field in the centre of the village became a village green, and a cricket and football pitch along with a sports and social club were developed. Change continued to be felt, as one of the pubs closed down, the coalman and the milkman stopped coming to the village and the tiny school became a house, to be replaced by a shiny new school. No farms meant there were no horses, and no horses meant there was no longer any need for a blacksmith/farrier. Next to the blacksmith, the farm housing the milking shed and barn for the bull became a site for four new bungalows. Eventually the village store and post office also closed. The village church, however, benefitting from the influx of new homes being built and has flourished, with a succession of hardworking, well-respected ministers. Though many of the old thatched cottages have also gone over the years, a few remain. Despite these changes, Bradwell village remains a small, charming, active community.

🍁 BRILL

Brill, some four miles north west of Long Crendon, stands on a hilltop with magnificent views over Aylesbury to Calvert and over Oxfordshire to the Cotswolds.

A 17th-century windmill, which is open to visitors in summer, dominates the common. Many years ago, the common was quarried, hence the deep undulations. Villagers have the right still to graze sheep on this, and in times past refused to have the ground levelled as it would reduce the area of grass.

Cottages are set around a delightful village green. Nearby is the 12th-century church with its 15th-century tower. The local Memorial Hall plays host to fitness classes, film nights and toddler groups.

🍁 BUCKLAND

Buckland is a village and civil parish in Aylesbury Vale district in Buckinghamshire. The village had a WI and a women's cricket team in the 1930s! Howzat for equality? Buckland seems to have had its fair share of notable residents, but the most eccentric and interesting appears to have been Miss Isabel Fry. Miss Fry, who was part of the Fry's Chocolate family and a Quaker, opened an experimental school in Buckland in 1934 for deprived children and refugees. Older residents of Buckland remember her each month giving the children of the village a bar of chocolate, or if it was Easter a chocolate egg – Fry's of course.

🍁 CHALFONT ST GILES

Chalfont St Giles lies about three miles south east of Amersham. A classic English village, it has a pretty church, pond and village green surrounded by cottages. There is a Roman road running through it, so the village boasts nearly 2,000 years of history.

The church was built in Norman times and the dedication to St Giles may possibly refer to the beechwoods that once covered the surrounding hills, St Giles being the patron saint of woodlands, as well as the sick,

Brill Windmill

poor, lepers and disabled. The east window of the church is said to have been damaged by Cromwell's cannon stationed in Stone Meadow while Cromwell himself was lodged at Stone House during the English Civil War. The River Misbourne flows through Stone Meadow and local folklore suggests that if it stops flowing, disaster will occur.

The principal great house of St Giles is The Vache, a very ancient manor house. The de la Vache family, once owners of the manor, may well have brought the name with them from Normandy when they came to England with William the Conqueror. The property passed later to Thomas Fleetwood, Master of the Mint to Queen Elizabeth I, and was held by that family until George Fleetwood, one of the judges who put Charles I to death, was evicted after the Restoration in 1660. The Vache was bought by Admiral Sir Hugh Palliser in 1771 and he erected a monument there to his friend Captain James Cook after the explorer died in 1779.

Between St Giles and St Peters on the north side of the Misbourne valley is another great house, Newlands Park. It was constructed by a Georgian banker, Abraham Newlands, who eventually became Chief Cashier of the Bank of England. At that time all bank notes were signed by hand and since Mr Newland's signature appeared on £5 notes, they were popularly known as 'Newlands'.

Chalfont St Giles is principally known for Milton's cottage, although the writer never actually owned it. When the Plague came to London in 1665, John Milton asked his friend and former pupil, Thomas Ellwood, to find him a refuge. Ellwood rented the cottage on Milton's behalf and during a visit Milton is said to have handed him the manuscript of *Paradise Lost*, asking for his opinion. Ellwood is said to have handed it back with the words 'Thou has said much here about Paradise lost, but what has thou to say of Paradise found?'. Legend relates that Milton later returned to London and wrote *Paradise Regained*. The cottage is now the only existing building in which Milton is known to have lived and is open daily to visitors in the spring and summer.

On the hillside above Chalfont St Giles is an obelisk some 60 feet high made of flintstones with the corners strengthened by brick. Although the obelisk itself gives no clue as to why it is there, local legend has it that at this spot King George III, being out hunting and separated from his attendants by a sudden fog, accosted a yokel and asked where he was. The yokel replied that 'Peters is down there and Giles over yonder but this 'ere ain't rightly a place at all'. To which the King replied: 'We will make it a place then.' He had the obelisk erected to mark the spot.

🍁 CHALFONT ST PETER

The village of Chalfont St Peter is special because of its location in a valley in the Chiltern Hills that was scoured away in the Ice Age millions of years ago. The River Misbourne, a chalk stream, and one of very few in the country, runs spasmodically through and under the village, and is monitored and cared for by a local team of volunteers.

Chalfont St Peter was on the old coaching route to London. Now, the A413 follows a similar route skirting the edge of the village.

In the village, The Greyhound Inn, which dates from 1780, stands beside the parish church of St Peter, and along Church Lane is the much loved village school – so popular it has had to expand well beyond its original Victorian limits. Fields and allotments run nearby and walking along the valley here, through miles of fields and away from the traffic, is a joy.

The church hall and the community centre, built after much fund raising are both enormous assets to those in the village, and are used by all age groups from a flourishing U3A to baby and toddler groups and, of course, the WI.

The Annual Feast Day, which dates from 1229 when it was conferred by the Lord of the Manor, celebrates St Peter's Day each June and attracts many hundreds of people who enjoy the numerous stalls, school

Chalfont St Peter Market Place

performances and a variety of colourful displays. Fun Night in December transforms Market Place with lights and stalls and a funfair.

The WI joins the Remembrance Day Parade each year in respect for the many local fallen. Two local residents won Victoria Cross medals and many other brave and gallant men are remembered in a special area in St Peter's Garden.

Flags are flown along Market Place and High Street for all special occasions, engendering a real feeling of involvement throughout our community.

A splendid series of oval plaques have been erected around the village, illustrating the history of the area. These make up a trail to follow of about 40 plaques making a fascinating walk of about two hours.

However, one of the most special things about Chalfont St Peter is the people. There is such a feeling of community and friendliness. Volunteers keep the library, charity shops and local events flourishing. All in all, it is a very special village.

🍁 CHEARSLEY

The village of Chearsley is a small village on the Buckinghamshire/ Oxfordshire border. The village is bordered by the Thame/Aylesbury road, from where the pretty, traditional sunken lanes meander downhill towards the church and the river. These lanes have been carved out by the cartwheels, livestock and generations of footsteps made by Chearsley folk over many years.

The hub of the village is the village green, wrapped around by traditional cottages, the Bell village pub and the village shop. This is the heart of the village where people meet and chat over a bottle of milk or a pint of beer, new friendships are made and old ones nurtured. The pub and shop have changed hands over the years, but with village support both are still going strong.

Many a celebration has been hosted on the green, including barbeques and village fetes.

The village is also host to numerous other events such as rounders matches, pram races, men versus women cricket matches, bonfire nights and the yearly tug of war across the river against the neighbouring village of Cuddington, where most competitors usually end up in the river – any excuse to have a fun time in Chearsley.

One image never to be forgotten was of Chearsley children gently floating across the local fields on every inflatable craft imaginable when the river had burst its banks and flooded the surrounding area, a pretty normal day in the life of Chearsley folk.

St Nicholas church in Chearsley provides the bedrock of life in the village. This 12th-century church has a special place in the hearts of many of the villagers. The churchyard is a carpet of snowdrops in spring, softly guarding all those who have gone before. The new church bells, the pride of hardworking fundraisers, ring out to call the congregation, old and young, to join in prayer and praise. This small, ancient, beautiful church is a peaceful place to just sit and watch the sun stream through the windows and enjoy the silence. It has been described as feeling like someone is wrapping a warm blanket around you as you walk through the door.

Beside the church lies one of the local farms, once a pick-your-own fruit farm employing local people to grow, nurture, pick and sell its fresh fruit to the local community. Sadly this has had to close but there was nothing better than sitting in the sunshine, chatting to neighbours whilst eating far too many strawberries.

There have been many groups, clubs and activities in Chearsley over the years, from lace-making in 1890 to ladies' Morris dancing in more recent years. The Cherry Bumpers group was created and managed to dance their way round most of the local public houses. The name gives a clue to the standard of dancing, but it was thoroughly enjoyed by everyone.

A popular present day get-together is the weekly Friday morning coffee and cake in The Bell pub. Lovely home-made cakes and as much coffee as you can drink, in the company of as many villagers who can squeeze into the pub, makes this a morning to look forward to.

Another thriving activity in Chearsley is at the village cricket club. Revamped in the 1980s to provide an activity for a glut of small boys prevalent in the village at that time, a junior cricket team was launched. Land for a new pitch was agreed with the local farmer and, with the help of some enthusiastic fathers (in some very dubious old cricketing attire), the new joint senior and junior club was formed. The club has gone from strength to strength, with a new pavilion, regular league matches and now with girls in the team.

Chearsley has produced many colourful characters over the years, all contributing to village life's rich tapestry. A local hangman found his home in Chearsley in 1900 and an unfriendly poltergeist called Old George had to be forcibly removed from a local property by the then local priest. An eccentric vicar prone to wearing three hats at once, outrageous actors, shop-keepers risking life and limb using a demon bacon slicer and finger snatching Arkwright's till, have all played their part in Chearsley's colourful life, to mention just a few!

It was a sad day in Chearsley when we lost our fight to keep the village school open. Despite all our efforts, the doors had to be closed. Fortunately the village children are now happily settled in surrounding village schools and life goes on. CHUF, the under-fives pre-school is still going strong, providing laughter and learning for the little people and is now settled into the new village hall. Several years of hard work and fund-raising has resulted in a brand new building for the village hall. The WI now meets in the new hall but some feel just a little nostalgic over the demise of the old village hall, a building which could tell many a tale, and make many a villager blush! However, the hall and the village must move forward together. New homes are being built, new families are moving in and Chearsley will grow and move with the times. Its heart will continue to beat loud and strong and will embrace the future with love and laughter, just like it has always done in the past.

🍁 CHEDDINGTON

With its very own railway station on the main line into London, Cheddington provides a perfect link for commuters and pleasure-loving villagers to the capital's theatres, museums, shops and restaurants in just 40 minutes. Sadly, in 1953 the branch line to Aylesbury was axed. This had been used by villagers to access hospitals in Stoke Mandeville and Aylesbury at a cost of sixpence ha'penny return! The line became infamous in 1963 when at 3.00 am on August 8th a gang brutally robbed a Royal Mail train just outside the village. The Great Train Robbery has been dramatized in a full-length film and a TV series. It should have been carrying £300,000 but due to a bank holiday in Scotland it was carrying £2.6 million which the robbers grabbed in cash. In today's market, it would be worth £48 million.

The trains also played a major role before the Second World War in transporting plums to London, which grew in profusion on the south facing slopes beneath the church. Eventually the cost of labour became higher than the price received for the plums, so the trade ceased. Many different types of plums were grown, including damsons which were used as dyes for uniforms during the First World War. Apples were also grown there, and the old trees still stand in military formation flanking the footpath up to St Giles church. The path is a delightful well-used walk through the orchards, set in fields of grass continuing upwards into the closeness and wildness of blackberry brambles and overgrown trees and bushes, at times alive with birdsong and the buzzing of bees before it meets a wooden kissing gate into the churchyard. In a quiet grassy area stand three distinctive Celtic stone crosses marking the resting place of three children, all from one family. Alfred aged 6, Thomas 11 and Elizabeth 13 probably died of cholera or smallpox. Their parents, Thomas and Marianne lost Alfred in 1856 and Thomas and Elizabeth in 1859, just two days apart.

Today young families are abundant in the village. The school is full and there are many excellent groups and activities. The annual fete on The Green in June throngs with babies, enquiring toddlers and busy parents joining in with all age groups. In November a large group of children join the annual Remembrance Service by the war memorial proudly wearing the uniforms of the groups they belong to. They place poppy wreaths in honour of locals who fought in the wars and in doing so, show respect for the past and hope for the future.

The plums have gone, although they remain as memories, but the families are thriving and keeping the village forever growing.

🍁 CHESHAM BOIS

Chesham Bois village lies between the towns of Amersham and Chesham, and today could be considered a suburb of Amersham on the Hill; the gradual dilution of identity as a village has been happening since the arrival of the railway to Chesham in 1889 and Amersham in 1892. It brought rapid changes to the area; many new homes were built, and an influx of shops and residents appeared around the new railway stations.

The history of Chesham Bois is closely linked to the Manor of Chesham Bois, its owners, and the farms and mills on the estate. Sir Thomas Cheyne purchased the Manor in 1446; he was a Lollard and spent time in the Tower for his beliefs. In 1738, the Manor passed to the Russell family who became the Dukes of Bedford.

Chesham Bois – St Leonard's Church

Villages need focal points; usually a church, a public house or shops. The chancel of St Leonard's Church, originally the Manor's chapel, has been a feature of the village since the 11th century. The Unicorn public house, backing onto the River Chess, was first recorded in 1770, closing in 1990 to later become a day nursery. It has been the only public house to have existed in Chesham Bois. At the turn of the 20th century there was a grocer, a baker, a dairy and briefly, a post office.

Much of Chesham Bois lies within a Conservation Area, which protects it from overzealous development and modernisation. With a considerable amount of woodland within the boundary, visitors think the name 'Bois', pronounced 'boys', refers to the French for wood. In fact, Bois is believed to derive from the Norman 'de Bois' family who were lords of the Manor in the 11th century. The woodlands, coupled with the Common and its pond, are a significant amenity – contributing to the character of the village and its history. Much of the current beech woodland was planted to support a thriving brush making industry in Chesham in the 1890s. This industry petered out, leaving Chesham Bois with lots of trees of a similar age which, because they were planted as a crop, are too close together to be sustainable without intervention. The Woodland Trust now manages the woodlands to ensure succession.

In beautiful surroundings, Chesham Bois has had its own burial ground from 1924, extended in 2007 to incorporate woodland burials. Whilst mostly a quiet village, it didn't escape war damage when a German V1 rocket landed here during WW2, demolishing a house.

For its size, Chesham Bois has had several prominent residents – artistic, brave and innovative.

Louise Jopling Rowe was an artist. She founded the Chiltern Club of Arts & Crafts after moving here in the early 1900s. She was a very successful painter and writer, born in 1843, a time when British women and girls were legally still the property of husbands or fathers. The 90 years of her fascinating life spanned a period of unbelievable change and by the time of her death in 1933, British women had at last gained the vote. As a supporter of the National Union of Women's Suffrage this would have been hugely important to her.

Lt Cdr Peter Scawen Watkinson Roberts RN (1917 to 1979) was awarded the Victoria Cross in 1942. The submarine HMS *Thrasher*, attacked off Crete on 16 February 1942, was subjected to a three-hour depth charge attack and aerial bombing. After surfacing, two unexploded bombs were discovered in the gun-casing. Lieutenant

Chesham Bois – Anne's Corner

Roberts and Petty Officer Gould removed the first bomb, but the second had penetrated the side plating of the gun emplacement. Petty Officer Gould, with a 100 lb bomb in his arms, was dragged along the casing by the shoulders by Lt Roberts and the bomb was dropped over the side.

Caroline Richardson, an artist, also belonged to the Chiltern Club of

Arts & Crafts and ran Red Cross working parties from the home she shared with her sister Josephine during both World Wars. When Queen Elizabeth visited the area in 1941, she met Josephine and Caroline in recognition of their work for the Red Cross. We know the Queen also met the local Women's Institute at Hyde Heath. The WI movement was founded in 1915 and despite the Hyde Heath WI also being established in 1919, the movement was still in its infancy in the locality; Chesham Bois had to wait until 1970 for its own branch.

Edmund Crispin, the pseudonym of Bruce Montgomery (1921–78), author of the Gervase Fen novels and a composer of film scores, lived here.

Mervyn King – former Governor of the Bank of England – was born in Chesham Bois in March 1948, but moved away before he started school.

Dame Stephanie Shirley, known as Steve – it was easier to succeed in business during the 1960s if you were a man – is a retired business woman and philanthropist. In 1962, she founded Freelance Programmers. Most of her IT specialists were women with dependents who were unable to work in a conventional office environment; the company pioneered flexible contracts and working from home. The Shirley Foundation now also supports research into all aspects of autism spectrum disorders.

Along with Chesham Bois residents, the Parish Council works to keep a village identity, publishing its own magazine *Bois Own*, facilitating fetes and picnics on the Common and Remembrance Day parades. Award-winning family butchers, Mayo Bros, have been in the village since the 1930s and there is still a well-stocked, and well-used, grocery.

A junior school, nursery schools, two independent schools, together with Scouts and Brownies, all manner of sporting clubs and Chesham Bois WI, add to a lively community. Chesham Bois WI, 50 years 'old' in 2020, continues to support village activities, recognising that the area remains a particularly splendid part of the Chiltern Hills.

🍁 CHOLESBURY-CUM-ST LEONARDS

Situated in the Chiltern Hills, to many people the parish of Cholesbury-cum-St Leonards (which includes Hawridge and Buckland Common as well as Braziers End, Heath End and The Vale) may appear as a rural backwater. It certainly seems that way when directions have to be given to speakers wishing to find our two village halls. The narrow twisting roads and hills can be quite daunting, especially at night.

However, our proximity to London has made this area a popular place in which to live. In the past it was equally popular as a summer or weekend retreat for city dwellers, especially as the London line to Chesham, and the main line through Tring, are both only five

Cholesbury

miles away; an important consideration before cars were so numerous.

In fact, the connection with London goes back even earlier. In the 16th century Daniel Bachelor, whose family lived at Chapel Farm in St Leonards, became a lutenist in the court of Queen Elizabeth I. Then in the 19th century, Cholesbury resident David Newton joined the Royal Marines at Chatham and fought at the Battle of Trafalgar. He married his wife in 1816 in St Andrew's Church, Holborn. Newton returned to Cholesbury and lived to the age of 99 and is buried in the churchyard.

In the early 20th century the author Gilbert Cannan and his wife, Mary, took up temporary residence here at our local landmark, the Windmill in Cholesbury, where they were visited by many other authors and members of the literary world, including Katherine Mansfield and John Middleton Murry, Sir Compton Mackenzie and Lytton Strachey (with D H Lawrence and his wife Frieda just around the corner in Bellingdon).

At the same time, the artists Mark Gertler and Dora Carrington were frequent visitors. Gertler is well-known for his First World War painting *The Merry Go Round* and his dramatic painting of *Gilbert Cannan and his Mill* at Cholesbury, with its portrayal of Porthos, the black and white dog, on whom J M Barrie modelled Nana in *Peter Pan*.

After the Cannans left the Mill in 1916 it was rented for a time by the American actress Doris Keane while she was appearing in the London theatre. Part of a wooden frame was recently found in an outbuilding of a nearby house with the inscription "Doris Keane in 'Romance' by Edward Sheldon". Artistic and theatrical connections continued. In the 1930s, Bernard Adams, RA, a Chelsea landscape and portrait artist who came out to live in Buckland Common during the summer months, held an art school in the windmill. Later, in the 1960s, Don and Maisie Saunders bought the mill and restored the sails. Maisie was a former Tiller Girl. Continuing the connection, Sir David Hatch, radio comedian known for *I'm Sorry, I'll Read That Again* amongst other series and later Controller of Radio 4, lived at the Mill.

Other actors of stage, film and TV screen who have lived here include Jean Rooke, wife of fellow actor Milton Rosmer. Margaretta Scott and her husband, the film composer John Wooldridge, also lived in Hawridge. Their daughter, Susan, continues in the acting tradition. The area is still popular with people involved with stage and screen. There are many film location finders, television presenters and personalities living here today.

As a further literary connection, the journalist and the first, and longest, serving editor of *The Times* crossword puzzle, Ronald Carton, was living at Cholesbury just before the outbreak of the Second World War.

Horace Brackley's family were certainly not summer or weekend visitors but yeoman farmers here in St Leonards for more than 300 years. Horace was a talented artist who served abroad in the Second World War and depicted scenes from those years together with producing many fine sketches and drawings of the local area.

Over the years there have not been many changes to this Area of Outstanding Natural Beauty. The commons and the beech woods, and the many footpaths, have been enjoyed and appreciated and continue to be so to this day by both the residents of the parish and visitors who come out by foot, bicycle, car and train.

THE CLAYDONS

The Claydons are made up of three villages; East Claydon, Botolph Claydon and Middle Claydon. The name Claydon derives from the Old English 'claegig + dun', which means 'clayey hill'. The word 'Botolph' is from the Old English 'botl' and means 'house or building'. Originally the villages were surrounded by the royal hunting forest of Bernwood; remnants of the ancient forest remain and are popular with walkers, especially at bluebell time.

East and Botolph Claydon sit side by side while Middle Claydon consists mainly of farmland and lies closer to Claydon House and its Park, the home of the Verney family. Claydon House is now owned by the National Trust. Florence Nightingale was a regular visitor to Claydon House, as her sister, Parthenope, was married to a member of the Verney Family.

Florence was involved in the creation of the library at East and Botolph Claydon which was built in 1901. This is now the village hall and the hub for all three villages. It is where social events such as dances, films and the harvest supper take place and is where The Claydons WI hold their monthly meetings. The hall is situated next to East Claydon C of E Primary School, built in 1908 under the auspices of Sir Edmund and Lady Margaret Verney. In between the hall and school stands the still-working clock tower, built in 1913, which joins or separates East and Botolph Claydon, and has a face for each community.

Another significant local feature is The Mushroom Tree. The name derives from the old, living oak tree which has a thatched roof or canopy constructed above it resembling a mushroom. This was renovated in 2012 to commemorate the Queen's Diamond Jubilee. Surrounding the tree is a wooden seat, known as The Mushroom Seat, which acted as a spot to rest for villagers in days gone by. The ladies of the Verney family who resided at Botolph House were said to have rested there on the way to and from church to enjoy the view. Attached to the village hall now is The Mushroom Bar, named after the tree. Nearby is The Spinney children's playground, extended in 2011.

At the turn of the 19th century, most women were either at home or employed as domestic servants, postmistresses, teachers, housekeepers or laundresses, whilst the men were predominantly either farmers, agricultural labourers, or cowmen. The Claydon Estate also provided employment. But since the Second World War, the rapid increase in farm mechanisation, and the consequent decrease in the numbers of farm workers, has caused the character of these villages to change. Now many of the houses are privately owned and are lived in by people who commute to Aylesbury, Milton Keynes or London, or who work from home. Many people are now retired, and the majority of mothers work. The population is about 350 and the number of dwellings is over 160. The major employer is a pharmaceutical products company but there are still four working farms, an auction room, a silversmith, a travelling farrier and one enterprising man has set up and runs a successful children's nursery. In Middle Claydon, The Puzzle Centre, a specialist pre-school for autistic children, has run for several years. The railway station, post office and village store are long gone, and there is not a regular bus service. Delivery services such as butchers and greengrocers no longer happen, but milk and bread are still delivered, with glass milk bottles!

There are 28 listed buildings in East and Botolph Claydon, many of which are brick and timber thatched cottages. St Mary's Church was built in the 12th century and still holds regular services. The White House, originally the manor house, probably dates from the 16th century and is reputed to have a ghost. Botolph House, once the dower house for the Verney family, is Palladian style and was built circa 1750. The well-known architects Parker and Unwin designed East Claydon School and a further Arts and Crafts house known as The Emerald. They were both commissioned by Sir Edmund Verney. The unusual 1827 listed building in Middle Claydon (now the home of The Puzzle School) was originally The Park School for boys until 1900, after which it became a post office, and one of the first village lending libraries in the country, due to the financial help of Sir Harry Verney and Florence Nightingale.

Looking to the future there are several concerns for the parishes. HS2 will pass within three miles of the villages and a large maintenance yard is already under construction. In addition East-West Rail will create a

The Mushroom Tree, Botolph Claydon

link to Oxford and will cause more house building in the area. During construction, both of the above will have a large impact on our villages. There are also plans for an expressway which will carry traffic alongside the railway.

Despite these threats to the peace and quiet, there is still a good community spirit prevailing within the villages.

🍁 COLESHILL

Be careful driving through Coleshill, as you are liable to meet two ladies out walking a troop of deerhounds, or another group taking alpacas for a stroll! Sadly we no longer have the beautiful racehorses being exercised but there are still several ponies and riders in the village. On Boxing Day you need to beware of crazy amateur golfers merrily hitting balls towards the Red Lion Pub. Tower Road, Windmill Hill, Chalk Hill and Magpie Lane hint at an interesting history and lead towards a pretty Victorian church, a pub, an attractive natural pond complete with ducks and moorhens, a large village hall and an infant school forming the heart of this quintessential English village. There is another pub, The Harte and Magpies, situated alongside the Amersham to Beaconsfield road which is popular for wakes being not far from the crematorium, and the garden is full of happy families in the summer months.

The village's position on top of a hill, with natural springs providing fresh water, made this an ideal strategic place for early encampments and there has been a settlement here since the 6th century. The Domesday Book records eight farmers, but the name Coleshill does not appear until the 15th century. Coleshill is above the 500ft contour line and is one of the highest villages in the Chilterns. The common land at the centre of the village covers 25 acres and includes old chalk, gravel and clay pits, although the only reminder of the once thriving brick, tile and pot kilns is The Potters Arms in Winchmore Hill nearby. There also used to be straw plait makers, bead workers, lace makers, a blacksmith (Forge House), a miller (Windmill Farm) and a dairy farm. The village shop closed in 1989.

Historically Coleshill was administered as part of Hertfordshire despite being surrounded by Buckinghamshire, hence the name of Hertfordshire House. However, an Act of Parliament re-aligned the counties in 1844. This made it a safe haven for Quakers who met at Ongar Hill Farm. Later there was also a Baptist Chapel from 1859 – 1963.

The water tower can be seen from miles around. It was built in 1914 to raise the pressure in the pipes supplying water to the surrounding area from the reservoir which was constructed earlier, in 1895. In 1995 it was no longer needed and was sold, subsequently featuring in the television programme, *Grand Designs* (1999), as a single storey living area was built alongside, and again in 2009 when five bedrooms were added in the tower itself. A real treat for any Coleshill resident is to be invited to the top on a clear day to admire the spectacular views all the way to Canary Wharf. The windmill is less obvious but still easy to see if you know where to look. Called Grove Mill, it was constructed in 1856 (the walls of the first storey are 27 inches thick) and an iron great spur wheel on the first floor drove three pairs of stones. The sails were very advanced for the time and the miller could open and close the shutters even when the sails were in motion. The mill ceased working around 1903 and was later used as a meeting place for the Girl Guides, who met and sewed camouflage nets during the Second World War.

A clock chimes and you are drawn to the brick, stone and flint Parish Church. In 1860 the cost of the site and the building was £1,500. £200 was donated by the squire and interestingly his wife gave £100, and she laid the foundation stone. The west window was boarded up on the inside for blackout purposes during the Second World War and, as it was obscured by the organ, remains so over 70 years later! Newer additions include the Millennium Lychgate and the WI Bee Garden which softens the edge of the war memorial. Recently a beehive has been placed and successfully colonised in the churchyard. Every year there is a Pet Service (yes, the alpacas have been known to attend!) and there are beautiful Flower Festivals, one recently had a magnificent display of quilts too.

In 1992 Coleshill was designated as a Conservation Area and today has about 250 households. As smaller dwellings on large plots come on the market they are snapped up by developers and larger houses are built with smaller gardens. More sets of electric gates appear and inevitably the village becomes gentrified and less rural. Yet it remains a lovely place to live with bluebells in beech woods, arable farmland and beautiful countryside on the doorstep, and the main road linking swiftly to the motorways and Heathrow. A network of footpaths radiates out from the village promising tranquil walks including The Chiltern Way, which conveniently passes the pub. Most importantly the village is still a friendly community having a Village Day in July with stalls, music, children's entertainment and refreshments, and at harvest time a Village Supper is held in the hall. There is an active WI, Cricket and Tennis Clubs, Random

Ramblers, Horticultural Society, History Group, and Pub Quiz Team. The village hall, re-built in 1982, is popular with dance classes, Pilates, private tuition, bridge afternoons, a quilting club, the Magpie Club for mothers and youngsters, and many parties. These generate sufficient income to keep it in good repair providing a hub for village get-togethers, Parish Council Meetings and well-attended public meetings.

🍁 CUBLINGTON

There cannot be many villages in England that have actually moved, but Cublington has! It is situated in the Vale of Aylesbury and the earliest mention of Cublington is in the Domesday Book when 'Coblincote' consisted of 10 hides (1,000 acres) and land for nine ploughs. The property, worth £6 per annum, then belonged to one Gozelin from Brittany, a follower of William the Conqueror.

In 1322, sixteen households in the village were wealthy enough to be taxed but by 1341 when King Edward III imposed new rates on country parishes it was reported that about 100 acres of land lay fallow and uncultivated and 13 houses stood empty. The tenants, without the means to pay these new rates, had left the village. There were few lambs and sheep and not many households left to be taxed. This, along with the Black Death and badly drained land, meant the village went into decline.

By 1400 it had been reborn on its present site with a new church built in its centre. Many of the materials of the old church – stone and timber – were re-used in the new one and some of the fittings, like the old parish chest, were installed in the new church. This old chest – the oldest in Buckinghamshire – is still in use today. Furthermore a brass table in the chancel of the present church records the death of one John Dervyle who died in 1410 as 'the first rector of this church', his predecessors being rectors of the old church down the hill.

The old village site is still visible after all these years and is classified as an Ancient Monument. It lies in the field at the end of Ridings Way and has a footpath running through it.

Journeying today towards Cublington from Stewkley one travels along a switchback of a route lined on both sides by farmland, tall hedges and verges of wild flowers until one comes upon what remains of the Old Manor and its outbuildings. Built in the early 18th century the Manor

House was burned down around 1800 but the granary and range of stables and dovecotes, having stood empty and derelict for many years have now been restored to make two beautiful homes,

Turn here into Reads Lane, named after a local farmer, and then the lane leads out onto the Wing Road. It is just a short distance to the crossroads and it is along here one finds the village hall. Originally the village school, it was built with money provided by a generous local benefactor, Mr Biggs. It closed as a school many years ago but was re-opened during the Second World War to accommodate the many children who were evacuated to the village.

At the crossroads, obscured by a high hedge is the village pond. Before water was piped to the village women were known to have used the water from the pond for their washing. In those days, few houses had sinks and pumps were used for drinking water. An elderly inhabitant believed there are 22 wells in Cublington, most of which are covered by concrete slabs and a potential hazard for the unwary.

Times have changed considerably since the turn of the 19th century. The mothers were kept busy with their large families whilst their men folk worked locally on the farms. Young women usually went 'into service', often to other villages or Leighton Buzzard and almost all walked to their places of work. The village was quite self-sufficient with its own bakery, farm produce and a store but should one have needed to visit Leighton Buzzard, a carrier came twice a week to take passengers. There was poverty and hard work but a strong sense of unity and friendship.

One of the highlights of the year in those days was the Annual Feast with much eating and drinking and jollity. There were amusements for all ages and a wonderful day was enjoyed by all.

Described by one elderly inhabitant as 'a rather sleepy village' when he was young, Cublington could still be so described today but that, of course, is its charm.

❧ DENHAM

Since earliest times Denham has been owned or visited by many famous people. Connected for centuries to Westminster Abbey, Denham played host to visiting abbots and later, ancient Savay Farm became a convalescent home for nuns. It is pleasant to imagine the nuns sporting themselves beside the river as their health improved.

At the Dissolution of the Monasteries, Denham was leased to Sir Edmund Peckham, Master of the Mint to Henry VIII, and his son, Sir George, is believed to have entertained Queen Elizabeth I at Denham. If so, Sir George must have overspent on his entertaining, because his estates were seized by the Crown in 1596 for debt, and leased to Sir William Bowyer.

Great Royalists, the Bowyer family lost their fortunes during the Civil War and sold the Manor of Denham to Sir Roger Hill, who built the lovely Denham Place, at a cost of £5,591.16.9., between 1688 and 1701. The elaborate formal gardens were also re-modelled by 'Capability' Brown. The property was then acquired by a pension Fund of Allied Breweries who leased it to The Sheraton Hotels Management Corporation as their headquarters. In 1988 the lease was assigned to Rothmans International who then purchased the property in 1991.

While Denham Place was being built for him, Sir Roger Hill lived in Hill's House, a beautiful mid-17th-century red-brick house with Dutch gables, situated in the village street, close to the church. Hill's House was owned by Sir John Mills, the famous film actor, who could be seen on his doorstep every Village Fayre Day, presiding over his popular Bottle Stall.

In 1250 a charter for a weekly market and an annual fair was granted to the Lord of the Manor. The annual fair continues to this day and every year we enjoy stalls, bands, Punch and Judy shows, bouncy castles and roundabouts on the Village Green.

A quarter of an hour's stroll from the village green, back along the Pyghtle, takes a visitor to the oldest building in Denham – Savay Farm. Built on the site of the original Manor House, the farm was fortified and once surrounded by a moat.

Originally a great hall built on Sarsen stones with many very ancient timbers, Savay Farm has been added to over the centuries. At one time Savay Farm was a common lodging house, charging 4d a night without supper and 6d a night with supper, and the owner possesses a noticeboard requesting lodgers not to wear their boots in bed. During his Blackshirt days, Savay Farm was owned by Sir Oswald Mosley.

Not all of Denham is ancient. Close to Savay Farm lies our 'village within a village' the Garden Village of the Licensed Victuallers, of beautifully laid out retirement homes for ex-publicans.

Denham Village Infant School, in Cheapside Lane, is the original school for Denham, and has classes for Reception and Years 1 and 2. The school building dates from 1832 and is listed.

🍁 DORNEY

In the very south of the county lies the village of Dorney, bounded by the River Thames, which used to flood the surrounding farmlands, turning it into an island. The manor of Dorney is named in the Domesday Book and was famous for its honey – hence the derivation of its name from the Saxon 'Island of Bees'.

Dorney is three miles from Eton and approaching from that direction you must first cross Dorney Common, carefully avoiding the cows, whose grazing rights go back to feudal times. The Common is now enclosed by cattle grids, but in the 1920s there were gates, opened for passing traffic by a Mr Tugwood. There is a tradition that Queen Victoria's carriage once became stuck in a deep pool known as Lot's Hole, and she had to shelter in a cottage.

At the end of the village street is the main entrance to Dorney Court, the beautifully preserved Tudor manor house, which receives visitors from all over the world. There has been a house here since before the Conquest, and the present building dates from 1510. It was acquired by Sir James Palmer in 1600 and handed down from father to son ever since. The Great Hall, where the Manor Court was held, contains portraits of twelve generations. Sir James was Chancellor of the Garter to Charles I, and his son Sir Philip was a Colonel in the Royalist army, and cupbearer to Charles II. Philip's brother Roger was the husband of the notorious Lady Barbara Palmer, Countess of Castlemaine, the favourite of the King.

One of the bedrooms at Dorney Court was said to be haunted by a 'Grey Lady', but she has since been exorcised and is seen no more. Today the family still farm the surrounding area and have developed a new breed of sheep. The house is also a popular wedding venue.

Behind the house stands the parish church of St James the Less with its red brick tower. The church is 13th-century, but traces of an earlier Saxon window and door can be seen. Across the motorway, a winding old road leads to Huntercombe Manor and Burnham Abbey, both ancient sites still in use today. The nuns were turned out of the Abbey by Henry VIII, but the building survived and was re-consecrated in 1915 to become the home of an Anglican order. The farmhouse of the Abbey became a private house named The Chauntry and was the scene of a horrifying murder in 1853. The owner came home one night to find bloodstains in the hall and the mangled remains of his housekeeper upstairs. She had been battered to death by the groom, Hatto, after a disagreement, and the murderer was duly hunted, tried and hanged. Not surprisingly, this house is also said to be haunted.

In recent years, the name of Dorney has become synonymous with the sport of rowing. In 2006, Eton College built a 1.4-mile lake here for pupils to train on. Dorney Lake is now a centre for excellence and was used as the venue for all rowing events during the 2012 Summer Olympics.

⚜ DOWNLEY

Ivor Novello, the famous actor/composer, bought a house in Downley as a country retreat. Its rural peace combined with its easy access to the West End of London must have made it an attractive proposition. And let's not forget that the local chalk soil offers perfect conditions for Syringa so perhaps Downley was an indirect inspiration for his hit song, *We'll Gather Lilacs*?

The name Downley is thought to have evolved from two Old English words – Dun, meaning woodland, and Lea, meaning a meadow or natural clearing. Of course, 'downs' also means rolling upland, especially in the chalk areas of southern Britain. Downley, perched atop a hilly area between the village of West Wycombe and the encroaching sprawl of High Wycombe, certainly lives up to the latter description. This is why the locals speak of going 'up Downley', a phrase which has now been enshrined in the recently established village festival. Up!Downley, which incorporates the longstanding focal point of Downley Day, takes place on the Common over a 3-week period in June and covers all aspects of fun, music, art, dance and culture. Local groups perform as well as big names and rising stars of the comedy world. The whole community comes together to enjoy the entertainment and to share their own talents. The scarecrow competition certainly brings out everyone's creative streak.

Archaeological investigation shows there has been a settlement at Downley since Anglo-Saxon times. Its elevated position must have made it easy to defend. Agriculture would have been the mainstay of the settlers but in more modern times, Downley has been home to some industry. High Wycombe and its environs were, until the late 20th century, an important centre for furniture-making, particularly chairs. Downley had some factories in the village, as well as home workshops. The furniture-making firm Mines and West was based here too. Local legend has it that they constructed the dummy fourth funnel on the Titanic.

These days, Downley is almost purely residential and is a sought-after location, with a population of something over 5,000. Modern practice has seen the number of schools reduced, however, so that now there is only one primary school situated in the village itself. But the village has a strong sense of community and hosts a wide array of activities, including Tai Chi, Pilates, art classes, Assisted Scrabble, and French and Russian groups.

The Common is home to a beacon which is lit on New Year's Eve and other important occasions. There is also still a torch light procession to a great bonfire on the Common on the night of November 5th. Organised by the Downley Common Preservation Society, this is no ordinary Guy Fawkes event. There are no fireworks allowed. Residents make torches (basically tin cans stuffed with wadding soaked in some sort of fuel which are then attached to long sticks, as a nod to health and safety). These are set alight and carried in the procession. The early arrivals set light to the bonfire and when it's well ablaze everyone casts their flaming torch into the flames. The rationale for this wonderfully non-pc display seems lost in the mists of time but one local described it as having 'a pagan feel' to it. All that unbridled fire ...

A more modern tradition which has grown up in recent years is for the residents of Green Leys to decorate their houses with Christmas lights. With more and more residents of the road joining in year on year, this has become quite an event with a grand switch-on, on December 1st. Donations from visitors or passers-by are forwarded to local charities.

Like every community, Downley suffered the effects of war. 22 Downley men died in the First World War and in 1923 a hall was built in their memory with monies raised by public donation within the village. A further 5 men died during the Second World War and a plaque commemorates all their names. The land for the Memorial Hall was donated by Sir John Dashwood of West Wycombe Park, who owned most of the land around. Downley was very much part of the West Wycombe domain, though these days the National Trust is our 'significant other'.

The village of West Wycombe and West Wycombe Park itself, as well as Hughenden Manor down the hill from Downley (former home of Queen Victoria's Prime Minister, Benjamin Disraeli) all belong to the Trust. In the past, an aptly-named Coffin Lane led down towards the valley. Deceased residents were buried either in Hughenden churchyard or up at St Lawrence's churchyard in West Wycombe, because Downley straddled two parish boundaries. If the family could afford it, a local cart and horse would be hired to transport the coffin but if not, then teams of strong friends took turns to carry it. A hard and heavy load to bear.

There is a strong WI presence. At one point in the past, there were no fewer than three branches of the WI in the village. Pressures of modern living and the increasing need for women to go out to work led to the afternoon group closing but the two evening meetings continue and new members and visitors still join us for stimulating talks, activities and cake (of course).

Nearby High Wycombe continues to expand and assimilate its satellite villages and whilst, to some extent, Downley has fallen prey to that fate, it retains a distinct identity: its quarterly publication, *Downley Village News*, keeps residents up-to-date with a plethora of information about the village, and many of the residents are part of families who have been here for generations. But Downley inspires loyalty in the newcomer too. One only has to consider how house moves are often affected within the village because folk are happy here and they enjoy the intimacy of a small community. And they just don't want to leave.

🍁 DRAYTON BEAUCHAMP

Drayton Beauchamp, is known as the 'village that time passed by'. No pavements, street lighting, mains drainage, gas supply or shops. This settlement was in existence well before the Domesday survey, and over time county archaeologists have found Iron Age, Saxon and some Roman artefacts. During the building of the Aston Clinton by-pass, an early Saxon cemetery with 18 graves dating from around AD 600 was discovered. The 'Beauchamp' part of the village name refers to de Beauchamp – a family associated with the village from the early 13th century.

🍁 EDLESBOROUGH

Edlesborough is a village at the eastern side of Buckinghamshire. The name is Anglo-Saxon in origin and means Edwulf's Barrow. In the Domesday Book it was listed as Eddinburg.

A village wall hanging, completed in 1993, hangs in the village doctors' surgery. It was designed and stitched by members of Edlesborough WI and depicts significant buildings in the village. These surround a stylised map of the village.

The main feature on the map is the 9-acre village green which has a cricket pitch, football pitch, tennis courts and a children's play area. St Mary's Village Carnival is held on the Green on the first Saturday of July. This is one of the biggest local events and is run by volunteers. Part of what is now the Green was originally called Britten's Field. This was bought by 10 parishioners in 1966 to prevent the land being built on and extend the playing area of the existing Green. They were reimbursed by the Parish Council. The present pavilion is due to be demolished and replaced with a larger building with improved facilities.

St Mary the Virgin Church is a distinctive landmark at the south of the village and can be seen from miles around. The church was closed in 1976 and is now the responsibility of The Churches Conservation Trust. The ecclesiastical parish is now Eaton Bray with Edlesborough. It is the venue for the annual 'Edlesfest', a weekend of concerts and events in June and can also be booked for 'Champing' weekends. The Church used to house a unique rose brass, now kept safely at a bank. Its inscription, simply translated reads:

> 'What I spent, I have had;
> What I gave, I have,
> What I have refused, I am being punished for,
> What I have kept, I have lost.'

It tells us that John Killingworth died on 23 March 1412. An image of the rose brass is included in the badge of Edlesborough School and on the village sign on The Green.

Edlesborough School was endowed and opened in 1849 by the Countess of Bridgewater, who lived at Ashridge House. It had one room and a gallery. At first about 80 children attended the school but there were many part timers and absentees during bad weather. At the parents' request three hours were devoted to straw plaiting each day. The same building, with large extensions, is still in use today. There is now a pre-school on the site.

Near the school is a medieval moat fed by a spring. This is connected to fish ponds in the school grounds which have been restored and are now used for nature study. On the land inside the moat is a large brick dovecote in a sad state of repair.

On the other side of the moat is a 16th-century tithe barn. This has now been converted into offices. Experts date its construction to 1498. It is 180 ft long and 30 ft wide, constructed of oak and brick set on plinths of Totternhoe stone. The size of the barn gives some indication of the parish's wealth at this time.

There is no longer a pub in Edlesborough. The Rule and Square has been demolished and four houses built on the land, and The Bell and The Axe and Compass have closed and are now private houses.

Edlesborough WI was formed in 1929 and was originally Edlesborough, Dagnall and Northall WI. The members meet in Edlesborough Memorial Hall, where our banner is displayed. The banner shows a straw plaiter sitting outside her cottage and the blossoms of the Aylesbury prune plum around the border. During the 19th century Edlesborough was one of the many villages in the area which supplied straw plait to the Luton hat industry. Prune plums, which only grow in this area of Buckinghamshire and Bedfordshire, were transported to Covent Garden. They are harvested in October when earlier varieties are long finished and make good jam and wine.

Today Edlesborough is an expanding village with two new housing developments currently under construction. Most villagers have to commute for work but there are several small industrial units in the village. There is concern that the population of Edlesborough has grown too large to be considered as a village but many residents, including members of the WI, make great efforts to create a community spirit in the village.

✹ ELLESBOROUGH

Ellesborough is recorded in the Domesday Book of 1086 as Essenberge. At the census in 2011 the population of Ellesborough was 820 which comprised some 347 households.

Ellesborough is beautiful and is defined as an Area of Outstanding Natural Beauty and includes extensive, varying views of wooded countryside and rolling hills topped at Combe Hill by the Boer War Memorial, from where four counties may be seen. The spaces are havens for wildlife. The area is very popular with walkers and has many public footpaths including the ancient long-distance Ridgeway. Alpacas can be seen grazing from one of the footpaths.

HS2 will run through the parish and though it will have very little impact on housing – sadly it will have a major impact on the countryside.

The village has a brewery and a thriving pub, The Russell Arms, owned by the residents of the village. It also boasts a central, easily accessible and well-equipped village hall where the occasional barn dance is held, as well as quiz and curry nights, summer barbecue parties, harvest lunches, Christmas carol concerts and monthly coffee mornings. Sadly, there is no post office, shop or school now.

There are numerous buildings identified as architectural and historic significance, including Chequers, the country home of the Prime Minister. There is a great mix of housing with many smaller houses and cottages in the past having been used as agricultural and estate dwellings. There are several working farms in the area.

Our community is blessed with many local activities, societies and organisations, including a horticultural society, the silver band and a thriving Women's Institute which is closely linked with the neighbouring village of Kimble. We also benefit from an excellent village magazine which is published and delivered quarterly. Many residents open their gardens to the public during the summer on behalf of the National Garden Scheme and other worthy causes. Any resident in need may apply to Ellesborough Aid, or to the Ellesborough Relief In Need Charity.

The beautiful and historic parish church of St Peter and St Paul is famed for its beautiful location. There are extensive and idyllic views from where it stands on a small hillock above the village at the foot of Beacon Hill on the escarpment of the Chilterns, and it is at the centre of a conservation area. The building dates from the 15th century with indications of much earlier origins. The first recorded Rector was in 1223. It was extensively renovated during Victorian times and has an original Bryceson organ which has been in use for the past 135 years. A succession of Prime Ministers and their guests have visited and worshipped in Ellesborough church. Margaret Thatcher was famously known to have prayed there for comfort during the Falklands War.

Parishioners have planted hundreds of daffodils around the churchyard and wild flowers, butterflies and bees are encouraged by not cutting the grassed areas until the flowers have seeded. Cream teas can be enjoyed in the church every Sunday and Bank Holiday from Easter until the end of September. Thanks to a well-respected team the church bells ring out every Sunday morning, calling the faithful to prayer and on other requested occasions such as weddings and funerals.

And, yes, we have other famous residents besides the Prime Minister including former Formula One World Champion Sir Jackie Stewart and Sir David Jason who is very happy in Ellesborough and says he wouldn't live anywhere else, but, if visitors ask where they live – residents are sure to say, 'Sorry, we don't know exactly, around here somewhere'!

🍁 EMBERTON

The village of Emberton in north Buckinghamshire lies on the southern edge of the wide, lush water meadows through which the Great Ouse winds. The old coach road from Newport Pagnell used to swing between its fine stone houses and past its clock tower before setting off across the causeway and bridge into Olney.

Today, rescued by a by-pass, the village seems to the casual visitor a quiet and tranquil place, the clock tower still providing the focal point and parts of the ancient high street shaded with magnificent chestnuts, copper beeches and sycamores. But the quiet is deceptive. Though the number of its working farms has dwindled and lace making is now a hobby instead of an industry, Emberton is, underneath, humming with activity.

From what archaeologists have discovered there has been a settlement at Emberton from Roman times or earlier. The original form of the name was Eanbeorht's Tun, the word 'tun' meaning a farm. So possibly a Saxon of that name after crossing the North Sea, travelled up the Ouse until he found this good defensive position slightly raised above the flood plain of the river. The Norman conqueror divided Amberton, as it became known at one point, between the Bishop of Coutances and Judith, Countess of Huntingdon and from then on its manor was held by various great local families until it came into the hands of the Tyringhams.

For as long as there have been records the village seems to have remained remarkably stable. Emberton has always been dominated by farming and

Clock Tower 'Margaret's Tower', Emberton

remnants of the great ridge and furrow fields that surrounded the village before it was enclosed in 1798-9 can still be seen.

On the south end of the village, on a piece of rising ground, stands the Church of All Saints. It was built in the second half of the 14th century and was considerably restored in Victorian times. The chancel is said to contain the mortal remains of Sir Everard Digby of nearby Gayhurst, famed for his part in the Gunpowder Plot.

It was Rev Thomas Fry who gave the village its central focus today. Just below the church, where the High Street curves sharply, he built a clock tower in 1846 which he named 'Margaret's Tower' in memory of his second wife (he had three altogether). It replaced an old elm surrounded by a stone wall. The site had traditionally been known as Emberton Cross, indicating that a preaching cross once stood there. Today, the clock still keeps excellent time. The British Legion lay their poppies beneath its war memorial and the more robust members of the community dance round it on New Year's Eve.

Just before the bridge crosses the Ouse into Olney there used to be fields rich with gravel. When the construction of the M1 began in 1965, these fields were heavily quarried and left as an eyesore. However, two members of Newport Pagnell Rural District Council under whose authority Emberton then came, had a wonderful idea. They turned the scarred landscape into a huge country park with wildlife reserves, reed fringed lakes and open waters for sailing. This 200-acre park is still a popular destination today and welcomes visitors from miles around.

🍁 FAIRFORD LEYS

We are a very young village – built only 25 years ago. Some call it a housing estate but it is much more than that. There are around 3,000 people living in Fairford Leys which lies between the Oxford Road and the Bicester Road; the two are linked by Coldharbour Way (the only almost straight road in Fairford Leys). On entering Coldharbour you are met by signs welcoming you, plus flowers and signs directing you 'To the village centre'.

In the middle of the village is Hampden Square, dominated by a bandstand and surrounded by shops, restaurants (both Chinese and Indian), the church, the civic centre and the school. A wreath is always laid by the bandstand on Remembrance Sunday, there is a fayre in the Square each summer and mulled wine is sold at the Christmas Fayre each winter, when Santa visits and carols are sung. The WI help him by providing small gifts for the children. Last Christmas the church put on a nativity play in the Square.

The civic centre is almost fully booked with exercise classes and WI meetings on the 3rd Thursday evening each month. We meet, we talk, we listen, we laugh and we have a secret weapon called Beverley, who provides food at our social meetings.

The Square has planters on the bandstand, and by the shops there are hanging baskets which are a delight. At Christmas the trees and lights make it very beautiful. Walkways across the village and along the stream take you past children's play areas, bulrushes and small bridges, which add to the country feel. Seats have also been provided in strategic places. Even the main road, Coldharbour Way, is colourful with its bushes, hedges, trees and, in the spring, tulips and daffodils.

If you leave the Square past the gift/coffee shop, the public house and off licence you pass between walls and blocks of flats designed to look like a city wall. The trees have grown up over the years and provide a sea of colour. If you wish to keep fit you can join the walking club, or go to the gym, visit the football ground, or play golf at the golf club. You could catch our bus 'the silver rider' into town, passing the new sign thanking you for visiting.

You may still see Fairford Leys as a housing estate, but it's our village.

🍁 FINGEST

Fingest is a huddle of houses centred around the Norman church with its unusual saddle-back roofed tower. No doubt this community came into being here because of the several springs which are still around, which would have been a convenient supply of water.

The surrounding farmland is mostly chalky, but there is both silt and gravel close to the water sources. The poorer tops of the hills are rough pasture or woodland, mainly beech, but in more recent times some conifer has been planted.

Fingest Manor, of comparatively recent birth, is set on the site of an old abbey. There are stories of tunnels from the abbey to the church and of course ghostly ladies who roam around. The original name of Fingest Manor was Tingehurst which was once the name of the village. At the entrance to the driveway to the house is the old village pound. Stray animals were collected up and put in the pound and no doubt a fine of some sort would have been paid to get them out again.

Apart from the church, which is within the Hambleden Valley group of churches, the meeting place in Fingest is the Chequers Inn.

Early in the century it is said that there was a tiny school, run by the incumbent of the church, in what is now the old rectory. Alas there is no school now, nor even a village hall. How times have changed!

🍁 FLACKWELL HEATH

Flackwell Heath was a most unlikely site for the development of a village, perched on a high ridge between the River Thames at Bourne End and the River Wye in Wooburn.

It was essentially a stopping place for travellers and merchants on their way to Wycombe and the Aylesbury Plain. Given it was a breezy, heavily wooded area high above the Thames, with poor water supply, settlement was a slow process. It is thought that the first settlers were probably gypsies who based themselves in shelters in the Fairview Lane area. The names associated with this area, Chopstick Alley and Charcoal Bottom would indicate that they sold firewood and charcoal, and possibly some became bargemen.

Flackwell Heath provided shelter and accommodation for travellers bringing goods and services over the heath, and publicans benefited from the income to be made. Animals and goods came up Sheepridge Lane and then down Spring Lane or Treadaway Hill; Chapman Lane was probably the route taken by chapmen (peddlers who sold trinkets); Whitepit Lane was the route down to Wooburn. Gradually the population grew and by 1690 Flackwell Heath is a listed name in *An Alphabetical Table of all the Cities and Market Towns in England and Wales*.

The origin of the name Flackwell Heath is intriguing. There is mention of a Richard de Flakewell who had a dispute with Prioress Alice at Spade Oak by the River Thames. Another theory comes from flax which thrived on the hill, maybe pronounced as 'flack'; and another 'flacking', an old village word to describe the noise made by clothes in high winds. There are many theories!

Given its origins, unlike most English villages which were within one parish complete with a parish church, Flackwell Heath was divided by three parishes: Chepping Wycombe, Little Marlow and Wooburn, with no parish church of its own. Over the years this was made more complicated by the development of four distinct hamlets or settlements along the ridge: Heath End, Flackwell Heath, Sedgmoor and North End Woods.

The *Buckinghamshire Posse Comitatus Register* of 1798 lists the most important occupations in Flackwell Heath. Farm and market-garden work was high on the list. Lacemaking by wives and daughters supplemented farm work income. By 1800 many Flackwell men and women were employed in the 29 paper mills along the River Wye.

Flackwell's fame, or infamy, came as a result of the 1830 Wycombe Paper Riots. These events put the village onto the national scene where the 'Captain Swing' attacks on mechanising farming and local industries were carried out by labourers fearing loss of work. Rioters appeared in a courtyard drama in Aylesbury. Some 50 Flackwell Heath men were involved in machine breaking along the River Wye. Up at the Leathern Bottle in Heath End a trumpet call at the crack of dawn gathered the men who made their way down to Loudwater, joining some 400/500 from the Wycombe area who were headed towards Ash Mill, but when they reached Marsh Green Mill, the Riot Act was read and eventually the machine breakers were rounded up.

A Special Commission for dealing with rioters opened in Aylesbury in 1851. Here, 44 Flackwell prisoners were found guilty of at least one capital offence incurring a death sentence. Eventually sentences were commuted to imprisonment for 15 men, transportation to Van Diemen's Land, now Tasmania, for seven years for 27 men, and transportation for life for two men, although one of these was not transported probably because of ill health.

Frackle folk know how to have fun! For many years Cherry Orchards were a big feature of the village and source of income (including for children who were paid to stop the birds taking the cherries!). The Annual Cherry Fair was a big occasion with a parade of musicians and decorated floats, stalls selling cherries and much more. Today it is a more muted affair.

For many years those belonging to the Church of England had to go out of the village to worship. Consequently religious practice in the village was non-conformist. Flackwell Heath Infant school was opened in the Methodist Church in 1876. Eventually a dedicated Infant School was built on the site of the present Community Centre.

The forerunner of the present Christ Church (CofE) was built with money raised by public subscription. It was a small wooden structure with a brick frontage seating some 50 people and consecrated in 1932. In 1961 a stained-glass rose window was put into the brick frontage of Christ Church. Although some think it was designed by John Piper, it is more likely the work of local artist Patrick Reyntiens, constructed and assembled in his studio in Heath End Road. Now Christ Church is in its own parish.

When war was declared in 1914, Flackwell men volunteered to fight. Sadly many did not return. The War Memorial was unveiled by Lord Carrington (who owned much of the land around Flackwell), where 51 men from the locality were named, including Lord Carrington's son. From the school record we learn that many children skipped school to see a biplane that landed on King's Mead, and that they collected 240 pounds of blackberries for Army and Navy jam in 1917, an amount they exceeded in 1918!

In the interwar years change came to Flackwell Heath which had altered very little over the previous years, including plans to build council homes in the fields known as Grubbins Cowfield, but this was interrupted by the outbreak of the Second World War.

The village prepared to receive evacuees from West London and a volunteer Fire Brigade Unit was formed. However, war work was going on of which most were unaware. Major Baker was the Company Commander of the Local Home Guard, and lived in the village, but he also worked for the BBC and had been instructed to rig up an operational radio base at his cottage where he heard that the Germans had invaded Poland and therefore peace was at an end. The White House in Heath End was the home of General Sir Frederick Pile who was in charge of Anti-Aircraft Command from 1939-45.

Postwar, the population increased enormously, and a network of roads extended to the top of Whitepit Lane, and the building of the M40 in 1967 gave residents a direct route to Wycombe via Daws Hill. So from being a most unlikely place to settle, Flackwell Heath is now a highly sought after place to live!

🍁 FORTY GREEN

The tiny hamlet of Forty Green (originally known as Faulty Green) lies within the parish of Penn in Chiltern District and in 1875 consisted of only ten houses and the famous inn, The Royal Standard of England.

A building was mentioned on the site of this inn in documents when Penn Church (of Quaker fame) was dedicated in 1213 and was then called the Ship Inn.

When battles were fought in the nearby beech woods between the Roundheads and the Royalists, the inn became the headquarters of the Royalists and was called The Standard by the soldiers as the building stood on a hill. The story goes that King Charles I hid there. Certainly after the Restoration of the Monarchy in 1660, Charles II gave permission for the inn to be renamed and it is believed it is still the only one in the country bearing the name of The Royal Standard of England.

Forty Green is surrounded on three sides by woods: Corkers Wood – planted with pine, Roundhead Wood, and the largest – Hogback Wood which is now owned by the National Trust. The woods still show signs of the bodgers' work. The saw pits used by them are now playgrounds for children. In days gone by these beech woods were used to supply timber for the furniture factories of nearby High Wycombe. Part of the commuter belt, few residents work on the land and many are retired.

🍁 GAWCOTT

Gawcott or Chauescot dates back to the Domesday Book of 1086, and is just a couple of miles from Buckingham, the name referring to 'cottage for which rent is payable' – 'gafol' meaning tax/rent and 'cot'. Reference is also found to the Norse word for cuckoo – 'Gaukr' – pronounced 'Gawk'. Apparently the cuckoo was a frequent visitor to the west of the village until about 1940 when the area was destroyed during the Second World War making way for servicemen. The Cuckoo's Nest pub, previously The New Inn, in the west of the village closed some years ago, as did The Royal Oak, leaving one pub, The Crown. To the east is Signal Hill, a former MI6 intelligence station linked to Bletchley Park.

Gawcott is no longer a sleepy village outside Buckingham. Over the past 10 years young families have moved here, because of the good access to work in Oxford, Northampton, Milton Keynes and London. This, in turn, has brought children to the junior Roundwood School founded in 1839, now on a new site and joined with neighbouring Tingewick for the infants. The old school, a single storey building next to the church, is now a private residence and still retains the bell tower.

The Gawcott Gala was an annual event on the playing field with a BBQ, children's games and various attractions (helicopter rides one year) and an evening barn dance. This is now a smaller event – a traditional village fete on the green with a band, teas and stalls – always a happy time for the community. A progressive supper is another annual event, moving some 50 residents around the village into people's homes for each course – quite a logistical task for the organiser!

The village is surrounded by farmland. Some fields now have solar panels, a scheme in which residents were invited to invest with Gawcott Solar Farm. During recent years three small new housing developments have replaced Waglands, previously a small engineering business, now Gilbert Scott Gardens. The Guildford Laundry, starting in approximately 1903, was a big local employer, particularly when the business grew to include a contract with Stowe School (one resident worked there for 31 years) but is now Guildford Close, and Leyland Farm, once a livery stables, is now Leyland Close. There are some listed buildings including Old Eagles Farmhouse, home of farmer William Eagles. Gawcott was well known for lacemaking, employing nearly all the local women, with black lace being of particular interest. Lace Cottage is still standing.

The Richard Roper Playing Field has 11 acres gifted to the parish by Richard Roper, with further land added by the Faccenda family, providing cricket and football pitches and a range of play equipment. The pavilion provides a changing room, small kitchen and a meeting room, and there are plans to upgrade these facilities.

Gawcott was the birth place in 1811 of Sir George Gilbert Scott, son of the rector at Holy Trinity. He was a prolific Gothic Revival architect and designer. He was also the restorer of many churches and cathedrals, some of his best known designs being St Pancras Station and the Albert Memorial. His early career began as a leading designer of workhouses. His grandson, Giles, designed the iconic red phone box. The WI raised funds to purchase a refurbished box and convert it into a library for the village, and it now stands on the green. Holy Trinity's foundations were laid in 1802, but the building became unsound and had to be demolished. It was replaced in 1827 and in 2019 had major roof repairs. Pews have been replaced with chairs facilitating the use of the building for a variety of events such as quizzes, concerts, suppers and barn dances, while still retaining its main purpose as a place of worship.

According to George Scott there were a few eccentrics in the village in the 1800s – Zachary Meads was a 'sulky old giant who was never seen at church, or ever expected to do anything good'. Benjamin Warr had a 'sturdy' wife and, with a family of twenty children, filled one of the square church pews. Another character was 'Mother Warr' who kept a shop and did a good trade in lollypops, bringing them on stepping stones across a brook which ran through the main street, for children on the other side. Other, more recent tales, include sledging in a field down a big hill which the children called 'fat man's belly'.

The Chapel was founded in 1868 and continues to thrive with an excellent GIG organisation (God in Gawcott) running Sunday School and children's holiday activities. The village hall was built in 1924 from money raised at whist drives and dances.

There are 14 acres of allotment land which were donated by John West, a 17th-century benefactor 'for the benefit of the poor of the village'. These are now managed by Buckingham General Charities. Included in this area is Hodding Wood, previously allotments which were cleared and the wood planted for public use. Henry Hodding was chairman of the Parish Council and PCC (church council) and the instigator of the wood at the end of 20th century.

Chafor Vineyard is an award winning family-run 'boutique vineyard' on a 23-acre estate at the west end of the village (in cuckoo land!), producing excellent wines, some of which are now sold in supermarkets.

We are fortunate to live in a lovely part of the countryside and hope future generations will continue to maintain the village, not forgetting past times and its history.

🍁 GEORGE GREEN

Not a city, town, or even a village, George Green is described as a hamlet by many local history books, and this suitably describes it to this day. It nestles between Slough, Langley and Iver Heath in the South Bucks District.

From earliest records it is believed to have been named after George I (1660-1727). However, later records suggest that the hamlet was called Westmoor Green, but was renamed after the George public house, one of the local hostelries.

The land, together with the significant acreage of adjacent Langley Park, belonged to the wealthy Harvey family. In 1885 a plot of land was presented to George Green by Carolina and Diana Harvey in memory of their father Sir Robert Bateson Harvey Bart of Langley Park, and in 1892 they had the Harvey Memorial Hall built in their father's memory. To this day the hall remains a focal point and is used for ladies and children's exercise classes, a daily nursery/playgroup, a martial arts group, a model boat club, a social library, children's parties and a social garden. The WI also use the hall for their meetings. Outside on adjoining land, presented in 1947 to the people of Wexham by Robert P Morgan Genville in memory of Sir Robert Grenville Harvey Bart, there is some adult exercise equipment and children's play area as well as an outdoor table tennis table. The field is regularly used by a local school and is identified as the heart of George Green.

Until the beginning of the 20th century the land was used exclusively for agricultural purposes and very few houses or cottages existed. Next to the hall a school was built, but sadly this no longer exists and the Victorian building has been converted to a private residential property.

An increasing population in the 20th century saw the need for more houses and a mixture of private and council properties were built. The largest development by far took place in the early 1980s when plans were passed for a residential estate. When built, these properties sold quickly as they were attractive to those working locally on the large Slough Trading Estate and, due to their proximity to Heathrow, were also popular with airport workers and those commuting to London.

Despite a population explosion, it is surprising that no additional shops or local amenities have appeared. In fact, the only convenience store has shrunk and been made into two units. In the second unit a fish and chip shop is proving very popular. The local pub, the George, remains. However, local inhabitants have to travel to surrounding areas for schools, medical and retail services. A sign of the times!

🍁 GRANBOROUGH

Granborough was once part of the Manor of Winslow. A windmill stood on the hill in a field still called Mill Knob.

An older resident recalls the village in times past: 'Granborough in the days of my youth was a very friendly village, full of people of all ages, some very old. One thing which remains in my mind is the old ladies sitting in the doorways of their cottages, a shawl around them to keep warm and a pillow on their knees, making lace, without spectacles or any other aid'.

Most of the present-day inhabitants work outside the village, except those who work on farms. We once had a blacksmith, a wheelwright and undertaker, a coal merchant, baker, builder, post office and general store.

At one time the house known as Granborough Lodge, then the Vicarage, was supposed to be haunted by a vicar who died at Scarborough by drowning. Although I lived there for a number of years I never saw him.

During the war there was a day of fear and excitement when an American plane dropped a bomb in Church Lane which demolished the house of Mr W. Newman, our greengrocer, and damaged a few others.

There are a very few of the old families left now, but lots of newcomers, who we are pleased to say are very friendly and helpful, both in the church and in social life.

🍁 GREAT BRICKHILL

Great Brickhill is in North Buckinghamshire, 3 miles from Woburn and 4 miles from Leighton Buzzard, overlooking Milton Keynes 8 miles away. Bletchley Park, home of the Second World War codebreakers is close by. The name is of Brythonic and Anglo-Saxon origin. Both the Brythonic *breg* and Anglo-Saxon *hyll* mean 'hill'. In the Domesday Book of 1086 the village was recorded as *Brichelle Magna* because the parish had three manors. '*Magna*' became 'Great' in the 12th century.

The village is popular with commuters as Euston station is only 35 minutes by train from Leighton Buzzard. Rail links to other parts of the country run from Milton Keynes. Aylesbury, Northampton and Milton Keynes are other common places of work. There is a primary school and a pub but no shop although a fish and chip van visits weekly.

Various walks and bridleways connect with nearby Stockgrove Woods, Rushmere Country Park and the Grand Union Canal towpath. There is a cycle club, a cricket and social club, plus a tennis club with two floodlit courts alongside a multi-use games area and children's play facilities. The Parish Hall provides a venue for badminton, table tennis and short mat bowls plus facilities for a pre-school, Women's Institute meetings, a monthly book club and a small art group. An outreach post office and Citizen's Advice Surgery attend the Parish Hall on a weekly basis.

The village church, one of twenty Grade II listed buildings, is dedicated to St Mary the Virgin and is in a joint benefice with

Great Brickhill Village Church – St Mary the Virgin

neighbouring Bow Brickhill, Little Brickhill and Stoke Hammond. Originally a priory church of Dunstable Priory in the Middle Ages, the church was ransacked by a Roundhead garrison during the English Civil War and restored during the 19th century. The Hill's pipe organ, dating from 1875, is said to be one of the finest in the county. The church has eight bells. In October 2009 the original six bells and bell-frame were lowered and the bells re-furbished. The tower was strengthened and a new eight-bell cast iron bell-frame installed. Two new bells were cast and all eight bells were hung in the new bell-frame in 2010.

Behind the church was the original Brickhill Manor set in 70 acres of parkland surrounded by a high brick wall, now neglected and ruined in

places. The last manor house to occupy this site was built in 1835. In the 1840s, Lord of the Manor was Sir Philip Duncombe, a High Sheriff who became a baronet in 1859. He was a friend of Benjamin Disraeli who was sometimes a guest at the Manor. This house was eventually demolished in 1937 after serving for a while as Stratton Park Preparatory School. The Duncombe family remains in the village and still owns the estate, residing now in what used to be the Old Rectory.

Great Brickhill was drawn unwillingly into the English Civil War in 1643, when, due to its high position and proximity to Watling Street, the Earl of Essex's troops were positioned on the ridge waiting for the King's forces. The Earl stayed in an old barn with some of his army for six weeks. The barn was converted into two dwellings in 1967 and as such survives to this day near the Three Trees in the centre of the village.

At the Millennium a time capsule was buried beneath a large rock of local sandstone at the Three Trees. Amongst artefacts from other village groups it contains a WI programme, a photo of members plus a copy the WI magazine. Older village children now catch the school bus to Aylesbury from here.

Behind the Three Trees stands the Grange, previously known as the Lodge. It gained notoriety in the 1960s when it was used as a weekend retreat by

Cromwell's Cottages opposite the Old Red Lion pub, Great Brickhill

the Kray twins. In 1977 it was split into two dwellings, the Lodge and the Grange. The Lodge burned down in suspicious circumstances in 1988 but has since been splendidly rebuilt to match the Grange and the building is now a single large family home.

The Old Red Lion pub, opposite the Grange is thought to date back to 1577 and has changed little over time. It was frequented by the Kray twins and is now popular with walkers and cyclists due to its good food and the spectacular views across the valley from the garden at the back.

Another notorious property, near the A5 was an 'up market' brothel run by a woman called Sandy in the early 1990s. Fond memories are posted on the internet, commenting that it was very well run and discreet, where one never came face-to-face with another punter, although the car park was usually full. Others have mentioned skinny dipping in the pool.

John Horncap's Lane runs from the church towards Little Brickhill. John Horncap is thought to have been a hangman when Little Brickhill was an assize town notorious for hanging more women as 'witches' than any other assizes in the country. There were gallows at the top of the lane.

At the annual nativity, on a Sunday near Christmas, villagers dressed as kings and shepherds with various livestock, together with the vicar celebrate the birth of Christ. A village baby and its parents take the lead roles in a rudimentary stable furnished with hay bales. Others watch on, joining in with the carols, refreshed by mince pies and mulled wine. This is an excellent start to the festive season. Other annual events include a Church Plant Fayre, a Music Festival, Brickstock, and a Village Show run by the Garden Club. Such events bring the community together and make the village what it is.

At weekends Great Brickhill comes alive as a venue for cyclists, runners and walkers who revel in the challenge of the hills and the wonderful views across Aylesbury Vale, and take advantage of the many seats on which to rest and catch their breath.

🍁 GREAT HAMPDEN

Great Hampden is approximately 711 feet above sea level and lies about three miles south-east of Princes Risborough. It was formed when 'Hamdena' split into two villages in the 14th century – the other village being Little Hampden on the next hill. The name Hampden is believed to derive from the words *ham-denu*, meaning 'homestead-valley'. Grim's Ditch runs through the parish and is thought to be an ancient boundary from the Iron Age. In the 2011 census the population of both parishes was 300.

Great Hampden is scattered over a wide area with the church being half a mile or so from the centre of the village and the Hampden Arms public house. One hundred years ago the main industries were farming, forestry, and chair bodging in the surrounding woods servicing the furniture industry in High Wycombe. Nowadays inhabitants follow their own professions, be it in law, accountancy, property developing or banking and work in the surrounding towns or in London. The main landowner is the Hampden Estate with the farms tenanted out and specialists engaged to maintain the woods and carry out repairs to its let properties. There remains an active pheasant shoot which is leased out to a syndicate.

Hampden House, which stands next to the church, was once the home of John Hampden, who was made famous for refusing to pay King Charles I 'ship money' thus triggering the Civil War. It was the home of the Earls of Buckinghamshire until the 1930s, whereupon the house was updated sufficiently for a Mrs Robley-Brown to take up a lease in 1939 for a girls' boarding school. The school remained until 1980 when it sadly went into administration. After this there were a few short-term tenants, which included the producers of *Hammer House of Horror* films. The crenellations that appear on the introductions of the company's films are those of Hampden House. Hampden House is now used as offices and as a wedding venue.

The Church of St Mary Magdalene next to Hampden House is 13th-century, but much of it was restored in the 19th century. It celebrated its 800-year anniversary in 2020. Services are held every week and high calibre fundraising concerts are held annually. The concerts are always very well attended and seats often sell out well before the concert date. They have provided much needed funds to enable improvements to be made to the church. Recent additions include a kitchen and toilet facilities.

The Village Hall is just around the corner from the Hampden Arms and is home to the Great Hampden Cricket Team. The hall is used for regular Women's Institute and Parish Council meetings during the year as well as the Cricket Club throughout the summer. The Village Hall Committee works hard to keep the hall running for the community and holds twice-yearly quizzes to help with the running costs.

The WI is thriving. It meets on the third Thursday of every month except August, and holds monthly craft and luncheon clubs. The biennial Village Show is organised by the WI.

Over the years many famous people have lived in the parish, including of course John Hampden, cousin of Oliver Cromwell. John Masefield, who was Poet Laureate from 1930 to 1967 lived at Pond House for a period of time. He died in 1967 of an infection (he had gangrene in his ankle) and was cremated with his ashes laid to rest in Poets' Corner in Westminster Abbey.

Other people of note were Christine Keeler, who, it was rumoured, lived in the parish for a short time during the 1960s, and Sophie Dahl who lived at Pond House when she was a child. Rupert Brooke also frequented the Pink and Lily public house which is about two miles away from the village and where a room is dedicated to his memory.

The parish has been used as a location for various television programmes such as *Midsomer Murders* and *Poirot* and films such as *Cromwell* and *The Three Musketeers*.

> King Charles the First to Parliament came,
> Five good Parliament men to claim;
> King Charles he had them each by name,
> Denzyl Holles and Jonathan Pym,

And William Strode and after him,
Arthur Hazlerigg Esquire,
And Hampden, Gent, of Buckinghamshire.

The man at the gate said 'Tickets, please,'
Said Charles, 'I've come for the five MP's.'
The Porter said 'Which?' and Charles said
'These: Denzyl Holles ....'

In at the great front door he went,
The great front door of Parliament,
While, out at the back with one consent
Went Denzyl Holles ....

Into the street strode Charles the First,
His nose was high and his lips were pursed,
While, laugh till their rebel sides near burst,
Did Denzyl Holles and Jonathan Pym,
And William Strode, and after him
Arthur Hazlerigg Esquire,
And Hampden, Gent, of Buckinghamshire.

Hugh Chesterman

GREAT HORWOOD

My name is Rita Essam and I have lived in Great Horwood for 72 years, which I know is quite unusual as people tend now to relocate for employment. The population of the village is approximately 1050. There is also a large number of dogs and cats. At least half of us have one or two, which is great as there is quite a big dog walking community.

In this day and age when we are encouraged to take more exercise it is lovely to see families out walking across the fields. Sadly children are not allowed out alone in the fields anymore. When my brother and I were small we used to spend hours collecting leaves, sheep wool, wild flowers or making camps, climbing trees, and picking blackberries.

Great Horwood is surrounded by countryside and stands on a hill. The church tower can be seen from a distance, whichever route you take into the village. I remember an old uncle telling me what comfort he found in seeing his first glimpse of the tower as he returned after being away at war. The church of St James stands in the centre of the village on the Green which is surrounded by period cottages dating from 1781. The High Street is lined with period properties and we are lucky to have a large collection of thatched cottages.

Sadly we no longer have a village shop. However, we are only 3 miles from Winslow and are lucky to have a post office which comes to our Wednesday coffee morning in the village hall, and they also sell a few essential items. Often people with a glut of vegetables will donate them to be given away.

The village has two allotments, one located in Willow Road and the other in Church Lane where lots of hard work and chatting goes on.

Within the village hall there is a library and a jigsaw lending service. We have a number of social groups including Arts and Crafts, bell-ringers, and a very good Silver Band. The WI is a thriving group who organises lots of lovely outings and activities and has a Monday walking group.

There is a well run Parish Council that helps to keep the village running smoothly and attends to its needs. The village boasts two very good pubs; The Crown and The Swan who both serve excellent meals.

The children are very well provided for as there is a marvellous recreation ground, Horwode Pece, with lots of new modern equipment including a zip wire which is very popular. It stands in a very peaceful spot on the edge of the village and has a large picnic area suitable for all ages, 'oldies too'!

The Church of England primary school is thriving, and within its grounds stands the Scout and Guide headquarters, and they have all sections, Beavers, Rainbows, Cubs, Brownies, Scouts and Guides.

To the north end of the village sit the football and cricket pitches which have their own clubhouses. Both teams are well attended and very successful.

All these assets combined make a good village. However, what makes Great Horwood extra special are the people who live here. I know from personal observations that there is a genuine concern for the welfare of others. Good neighbours and friends are a great gift in hard times and good. I know that if I need help I could knock on any door.

As we move forward and welcome new people to the village I hope that we can continue to help and support everybody, as is the village way. There are things that have changed but not all are bad. May we embrace the changes and continue to be a caring village. After all, the sense of the past is always strong and long may it continue.

GREAT LINFORD

Great Linford village, with its 12th-century church and 17th-century manor house, is now part of the city of Milton Keynes, but still retains its village atmosphere.

The original village green remains, also a cricket pitch and several landscaped areas, all linked by the Redways (pedestrian and cyclist paths) and bridleways, surrounded by trees, shrubs and great banks of roses.

The village church is of great interest. Apparently, there was a chapel at Linford, on this site, in 1151. The church tower is 12th-century with various additions and alterations since. The 17th-century manor house was formerly owned by the Pritchard family. Sir William was a Lord Mayor of London and he also built the almshouses which are very attractive and now house various offices and artists' studios. The manor is now owned by Pete Winkelman, chairman of Milton Keynes Dons football club.

The Grand Union Canal runs to the north of Great Linford. It is quite widely used by barges, canal buses, the fishermen and busy families of moorhens. The towpaths have been cleared and it is pleasant to walk along them.

It is hard to believe that this lovely village is within a ten-minute ride of one of Britain's biggest shopping centres.

GREAT MISSENDEN

Following an excited crocodile of children down the High Street of Great Missenden, is not unusual. The village has all sorts of visitors, many come to the Roald Dahl Museum and Story Centre with its Big Friendly Giant decorating the outside wall. It's impossible to mention Great Missenden and not refer to the famous storyteller. Even one of the cafés is named 'Matilda's'. However, the village is much more than this.

With a population of just over 2000, it is a lively, attractive place, sitting in a valley surrounded by the Chiltern Hills. The River Misbourne, now culverted, runs through the village from its source at the Aylesbury end of the village. Many of the residents commute to London for work, by train.

The station, modernised but little changed since its opening in the 19th century, sits just above the High Street. Others work locally and many retire to the village, where farming still continues. Some families go back many generations. Sadly their family names appear on the war memorials in the High Street and outside the Parish Church. After the Second World War, many Polish families settled in the village.

The High Street is a mixture of all that local residents need, gift and dress shops also attract locals and visitors alike. At a glance, the buildings have changed little through the centuries, but the life they reflect certainly has. Essentials like the doctors' and dentists' surgeries, a pharmacist, post office, supermarket and library, provide the background to modern village life. At one time the village boasted nine pubs, nowadays it has five coffee shops and two pubs. Church life provides many activities throughout the year. A Roman Catholic church with resident priest as well as a Baptist church contributes much to village life. A regular weekly Lunch Club for the elderly takes place at the Baptist church and, along with the Roman Catholic church, many activities and events are provided for residents.

The Parish Church, dating back to the 13th century, and with a close association in the past with Missenden Abbey, is separated from the village following the building of the bypass in 1960. The church sits on the hill overlooking the village and is now reached by a bridge over the busy road below. Cream teas are provided by volunteers throughout the summer. Concerts and many events take place in this ancient church building. Its association with the Abbey goes back to when the monks provided priests for the church. Many stories are told in the village of the unruly nature of some of these monks. After the Dissolution of the Monasteries, the Abbey became a private home. In more recent times it has provided a grand venue for all sorts of village activities, as well as providing a home for businesses and education. Alongside the beautiful buildings is the recently resurrected walled garden. This is now run as a charity providing training and experiences for adults with special needs. Another successful Plant Centre also operates at this end of the village. The Abbey has always been a focus for the village and is probably how the first settlement grew up around it.

In the centre of the village is the Memorial Hall, built in the 1960s and providing for many regular village groups. Recently, a film club has been set up, showing films in the hall alongside offering refreshments. Flats for the elderly overlook the library and the hall and there is also an Abbeyfield home nearby. These buildings overlook the Buryfield, which is an open green space used for football in season and many other things, from village celebrations to large exhibitions, circuses and fairs. Each summer the whole area is taken up with Lighthouse, a Christian holiday week for children. Large white marquees arrive the week before in preparation for the hundreds of children who regularly take part.

As well as facilities for the older generation, the village has three schools. The original village school from the 19th century is still educating village children as well as those from surrounding areas. New buildings have been added, and it provides an excellent start for pupils in a beautiful setting. A successful secondary school, the Misbourne, is also part of the village. Its popularity means that many pupils come from out of the area. A small independent school at the other end of the village also brings more children into the village.

Great Missenden celebrates in many ways. Flags fly outside the buildings in the High Street and are flown on St George's Day and for royal events, as well as other occasions. At Christmas time, trees decorate the buildings. With their lights reflected all along the street, it provides a magical Christmas scene. In November, the High Street is closed to traffic for an afternoon and evening for a Christmas Festival. Fairground rides for small children, stalls of every kind, some providing seasonal refreshments are set up all along the street. Each year a wonderful fairground organ also provides a musical accompaniment to the excitement of the evening.

The High Street takes only minutes to walk, passing petrol pumps preserved from the last century. So many things take place here that it is impossible to reflect all that keeps this village alive. Its many attractions draw people to come and live here.

Previous residents in the area, have included politicians Clement Atlee and Harold Wilson. Actors and entertainers have included Geoffrey Palmer and Patricia Neale. The village has also been used as locations for TV programmes like *Midsomer Murders* and *Endeavour*. Village groups provide activities for all ages. For those lucky enough to live here, it is easy to take for granted our beautiful surroundings and all that village life has to offer.

🍁 GRENDON UNDERWOOD

Grendon Underwood is an ancient settlement, recorded in the Domesday Book as Grenndone, with18 households and a value of £7. In later years the spelling changed and was variously Grenedon, Gryndon and Grindon. 'Underwood' reflects the site's relationship with the Royal Hunting Forest of Bernwode.

For centuries Grendon Underwood was an agricultural community, and farming is still important to the local economy, alongside a number of small industries. The village has grown significantly over time and new housing developments are still being built, though many newer residents commute to Aylesbury, Bicester, Oxford, and further afield. Although all the pubs have closed, the church is still central to village life. There is a village shop cum post office, and a well-regarded village school. The large Village Hall was renovated and extended in 2003 after the Hall Committee made successful bids for grants from the Lottery Fund and Aylesbury Vale District Council, and is the centre of much social activity. A thriving football club, with teams of all ages, plays its home games on the playing field behind the Hall.

The most famous and probably oldest existing building in the village is the former Ship Inn, for many years a coaching inn on the London to Stratford-upon-Avon road before the A41 bypass was built, and now a private home known as Shakespeare House. In his biography of Shakespeare, 17th-century author, John Aubrey, relates that on one occasion, instead of staying at the inn, perhaps because he was short of money or there were no beds available, the playwright was sleeping in the nearby church porch. Here he was apprehended as a vagrant by two local constables. He may even have ended up in the stocks! The village constable at that time was Josias Howe, son of the rector. This incident is believed to be the basis for the characters of Dogberry and Verges in *Much Ado About Nothing*. A local wood is also said to have inspired parts of *A Midsummer Night's Dream* ('*I know a bank where the wild thyme blows...*') It is said that the ghost of Shakespeare can sometimes be seen at one of the upper windows of Shakespeare House.

Between Shakespeare House and the church is a housing development built on the site of the former Manor Farm (now demolished) which had its own well. In the 19th century, in a philanthropic attempt to improve the village's water supply, a local resident paid for a well to be sunk opposite the farm. Villagers were advised to

Be thankful whilst you fill your can
For God's most useful gift to man.

And below this pious admonition:

This well was sunk by Mrs Fitzgerald for the use of the parish 1861

Strangely, despite the good quality of the well water from the farm, the pump water was undrinkable and the well was never used. It is still there with its plaque.

A more recent literary temporary resident was Roald Dahl whose family moved to Grendon Cottage during the Second World War. He is still remembered by Pauline Hearne, who came to the village in 1946 after her marriage to Wilfrid, a friend of Dahl's, who like Dahl, had been in the RAF. Pauline took on the running of the Hearne family's shop, which sold boots and shoes. She extended the range of goods on sale to virtually anything inedible, including knitting wool, school uniforms, paint and DIY equipment. After the death of her husband, Pauline has taken on his role as Honorary President of the football club and is still an active member of the community and known to everybody. She joined the WI in 1946 and still attends regularly.

🍁 HADDENHAM

Modern Haddenham has a large and thriving community, likely to become even larger in the near future as developers build houses throughout the village. Despite the recent expansion Haddenham retains its village character and community spirit.

At its core is the picturesque conservation area featuring St Mary's Church, the village pond (one of several), the main village green and many listed buildings. Haddenham is especially noted for its 'witchert' houses, many of which are thatched. Witchert is a type of limestone clay found only in Haddenham and some surrounding villages. When mixed with straw and water, witchert has provided building material for houses still standing the test of time over several centuries. Many houses in Haddenham have 'secret' gardens surrounded by Witchert walls topped by tiles or, formerly, thatch. witchert forms part of the title of several organisations including our village Women's Institute, Haddenham & Witchert WI.

Haddenham is popular with villagers of all ages. Families are attracted to the village by its three primary schools, several nurseries and its proximity to places of employment, including an industrial area on the edge of the village. Relatively easy access to good public transport to Thame, Oxford and Aylesbury make it a favourite with working families. The Chiltern Line makes rail travel to London and Birmingham a viable alternative for daily commuters.

Retired members of the community find Haddenham a stimulating place to live. Indeed they are spoilt for choice when it comes to activities they can pursue in their retirement: U3A, WI, Probus, The Village Society, The Horticultural Society, Haddenham Players, Tennis Club, Walking Football, The 60+ Club, Monday Club, Church activities, and Art Clubs to name but a few. Not all of these clubs are solely targeted at the retired and several cater for the different age groups in the village.

Villagers do not have to look far afield for its facilities. It even has its own website, Haddenham.net, which is very popular. Unlike many villages it has not lost its post office, nor its library, thanks to a valiant crew of volunteers manning the desk and providing many other services such as IT help, booking for the Village Screen showings, and providing a venue for village events. Other valuable facilities are the village Medical Centre, Pharmacy and a community bus. Other amenities include several pubs, cafés and restaurants, a garden centre and a farm shop, both of which have a café. A wide variety of shops caters for daily needs. The Village Hall is central to the village; it has a large hall plus other smaller rooms. The Youth and Community centre provides another venue for hire.

The work of the church is also an important part of village life, with Anglican, Methodist, Baptist and Roman Catholic churches providing for all persuasions, the first three housed in splendid old buildings. For those interested in the village history, which stretches back to Roman times, Haddenham Museum provides a comprehensive display of artefacts from the village's rural past to its more recent industrial history. In particular First and Second World War memorabilia is displayed. During the Second World War, the village was home to the No 1 Glider Training School and the Air Transport Auxiliary, who ferried new and repaired aircraft around Britain. Each year the museum publishes the *Haddenham Chronicles* which comprises a series of articles about aspects of village history written by local people.

In common with many villages, Haddenham celebrates certain dates in the calendar in a traditional manner each year. At Christmas the mummers move from pub to pub to perform their traditional tale of *St George and the Dragon*, raising money for charity. On May Day the local children dance round the maypole on the village green. In June/July the village fete takes place on the village green and on adjacent streets there are stalls provided by local community organisations. September sees the historical Haddenham Feast, a funfair which takes place over the Church End area, after a blessing by the church on the rides prior to its opening. September also sees the annual Horticultural Show and December/January is panto time performed by adults and children from Haddenham Players.

In addition, special national events such as royal weddings and jubilees have been celebrated by local organisations with parades and street parties. In recent years the beginning and end of the First World War and VE Day have been remembered in plays and musical reviews, specially written to reflect the impact of the wars on Haddenham. For the past few years Haddenham Beer Festivals have taken place in both summer and winter and continue to be very popular, donating the proceeds to village organisations. No doubt more traditions will emerge in the future such as the Scarecrow Trail and taking part in these events is all part and parcel of being an established Haddenham villager!

We are fortunate in the village to have allotments and in recent years a community orchard has been established. Volunteers have planted, and maintain, a variety of fruit trees. On the outskirts of the village we have a 4.5-acre conservation area called Snakemoor, where you can enjoy the variety and changes to the flora and fauna throughout the year. Tiggywinkles is a long established hedgehog and wildlife sanctuary open to the public.

Sports are represented in the village with a tennis club, with its own courts; football and cricket clubs use the sports fields in the village centre and the old airfield site. Beavers, Cubs, Scouts along with Rainbows, Brownies and Guides meet in the Scout and Guide Centre, adjacent to the award-winning Fitness Centre.

All these activities, facilities, and community spirit come at a price: Haddenham is becoming an expensive place to live. It is, however, still a lovely, friendly place to live for young and old alike and we hope the next generation will strive to retain its community spirit for many years to come.

❧ HAMBLEDEN

Hambleden village rests in the centre of a valley that rises from the northern bank of the River Thames and runs up to the edge of Fingest in the heart of the Chilterns. It is 4 miles west of Marlow and 3 miles north-east of Henley and has a population of 1,413. The name means 'a village in a valley.'

On the river there is a lock and weir and a spectacular corn mill mentioned in the Domesday Book in 1086. This stopped working in the 1950s and has now been converted into flats. There is a large boat yard alongside. The remains of a Roman Villa were found in 1912 and some of the artefacts can now be seen in the County Museum.

The village centre, which is much photographed and appears in many films, consists of cottages clustered round an open square with its old village pump in the centre and the imposing church and lychgate to one side.

The village is very busy with a well-stocked shop and post office in the centre, a doctors' surgery and a builder. Sadly the school, the smithy, the baker and the butcher have all become private homes. The only pub in the village is The Stag and Huntsman, which also offers accommodation.

There is a Sports and Social Club in the centre of the village with a sports field for tennis, cricket and football. The Parish Hall opposite the church is well used for parties, social events and wedding receptions and by various organisations including the Royal British Legion, the Women's Institute and the bridge club.

The Parish Church dominates the centre of the village. A Saxon church was built here around AD 670 and the church has been altered and restored many times since. The present church, St Mary the Virgin, was largely re-built in 1859, apart from the west tower, which is older, although there are many features in the church from much earlier times. Some of the building dates from Norman times and includes a Saxon font, a remarkable D'Oyley monument and a new stained-glass window in memory of the 4th Viscount Hambleden.

The imposing Manor House, built in flint and brick like most of the cottages, overlooks the church and was built in 1604, with many alterations since.

Thomas de Cantelupe was born in an earlier Manor House in 1218. This was on the site of what is now Kenricks. He became the last English Saint of the undivided Western Church, becoming Bishop of Hereford

The old village pump
and the young oak tree
Hambleden

Hambleden village pump

Cathedral and Chancellor of England in 1265. His relics were kept at the Parish Church for some time but are now interred in a shrine in Hereford Cathedral. The link with Hambleden continues when the Hambleden choir sings in the cathedral once a year.

Many famous people have lived in Hambleden over the years. The son of the founder of W.H.Smith, the 2nd Viscount Hambleden, came to live in Greenlands, a large house, on the banks of the Thames, in 1871. By 1925 the Smith family had bought up most of the village, including the Manor House, where they lived until recently. Greenlands became the Henley Management College, part of Reading University. The Smiths were good landlords to the many estate workers who lived in the village and people were sad when they had to sell the estate. It was bought by a Swiss banker and has been amalgamated with the Culham Estate and the Deer Park in Fawley to become the Culden Faw Estate. Several of the estate cottages have been sold off and many people who live in Hambleden now are commuters, in great contrast to the past, when the vast majority of people

Hambleden church

in the village would have been employed on the estate, on local farms or as local tradesmen.

George Howson, the founder of the Armistice Poppy Factory after the First World War, lived in Colstrope close to the village. Robert Deane also lived in Colstrope. He was reputed to have signed the death warrant for Charles I, although the family dispute this. Thomas Moore of Hambleden was one of 37 Catholic MPs who withdrew from the House of Commons in the reign of Mary Tudor, rather than sanction her policy of religious persecution. In 1833, Isaac D'Israeli bought some land for his son Benjamin, so that he could qualify to become a Member of Parliament. However, when he eventually became Prime Minister, he chose to live in Hughenden and not Hambleden. Bacres House was the home of the 17th Duke of Norfolk for many years. James Brudenell, later Lord Cardigan who led the Charge of the Light Brigade, lived in the Manor House.

The War Memorial in the centre of the village records the names of 40 men from the village who died in the First World War and 16 in the Second World War – an amazing number for such a small village.

Many events are held in the village during the year. The Community Group organises a Bonfire and Fireworks event, which provides money for the over 80s Christmas Dinner and a Summer Outing. Various church events take place, including Harvest Festival when members of the farming community carry in sheaves of corn, which are specially grown and harvested locally. There is also a monthly Artisan Market.

Like everywhere else, it has become more difficult for younger people to live in the village, often where they have grown up and where their families live. Prices of property are high. Recently a Housing Association built nine houses, specifically for such local people but it is not nearly enough.

The village may look unchanged from the past but there is now much more of a mixture of incomers and locals which helps to keep the community thriving.

🍁 HANSLOPE

Hanslope is thought to have existed in Roman times. Coins and ornaments have been found in the area. It is mentioned in the Domesday Book stating that Aldene was Lord of the Manor of Hanslope. William the Conqueror later appointed Winemar of Flanders Lord of the Manor, who was followed by his son, then by William Mauduit – Chancellor of the Royal Exchequer. His sons, first Robert and then William, succeeded him. Robert drowned in 1120 whilst crossing the English channel with Henry I's children. William's son, also Robert, joined the Barons against King John.

The Mauduits succeeded to the Earldom of Warwick and in 1293 William Beauchamp Earl of Warwick, Baron of Hanslope won permission from the King to hold a weekly market in the village. The badge of the Earl of Warwick – a bear and ragged staff – can still be seen in the church.

The estates remained in Warwick's possession until 1488 when they were surrendered to the Crown. In 1663 King Charles II granted the Manor to Sir William Tyrell whose descendents sold it to the Watts family.

Edward Hanslope Watts, born 1845, was shot and killed by his gamekeeper in 1912 and his grandson – last in the line – sold the estates to Lord Hesketh.

In 1939 Hanslope Park, with its 17th-century manor house, was taken over by the Royal Corps of Signals and became a communications centre. Since 1945 it has been run by the Foreign & Commonwealth Office and is home to Her Majesty's Government Communications Centre.

Hanslope church

The Parish of Hanslope covers 5,290 acres. It is bordered on the north, west and east by Northamptonshire, and Salcey Forest is on the eastern border. The London/North West railway passes through on the west for 3 miles and the M1 goes through the parish for 3 miles to the east.

The church has one of the tallest spires in Buckinghamshire. Originally 206 feet, in 1804 it was struck by lightning and, when rebuilt, was reduced to 186 feet. It is topped by a weather vane depicting a hound with an arrow through its foot which was donated by William Watts whose life was saved by a faithful hound while serving as a Governor in India.

Joseph Knibb, a well-known clockmaker, born in 1640, retired to Hanslope from London and Oxford. He died in 1711 and is buried at Hanslope.

When Flemish lace-makers fled from the Huguenots, many of them settled in north Buckinghamshire. Hanslope and Stony Stratford became centres for the industry. In the 1800s, as many as 500 women and children were making pillow lace in the village.

There are many amenities in the village today, including a large recreation ground with football pitch, tennis court, cricket ground, children's play area, a sports pavilion and Baden Lodge (Guide and Scout hall). There is also Lincoln Court, council-owned sheltered accommodation for the elderly, where various activities are arranged.

A combined first and middle school was built in the 1960s. The old village school, once owned by the church, is now the Village Hall where many clubs and societies hold their meetings and which is home to the local pre-school.

The doctors' surgery is a great asset to the village. There are many public footpaths, including part of the Swan's Way, a long-distance bridle route from Salcey Forest to Goring-on-Thames.

For many years the railway works in Wolverton were the main employers. Nowadays, most people commute to work in Milton Keynes or further afield.

The population has more than doubled since 1960 when there were over a dozen shops and businesses. Today we have a butcher, grocers/PO, newsagent and a Chinese takeaway.

There used to be seven public houses and a Working Men's Club, but now there are just two pubs and a club.

Although we continue to grow in numbers, we hope we can remain a village and retain the community spirit that exists today.

Beaconsfield Old Town

Bledlow – Old Papermill

Brill Windmill

Chearsley – The Bell

Claydon's Mushroom Tree

Ellesborough

Great Horwood

Great Missenden

Haddenham

Hambleden

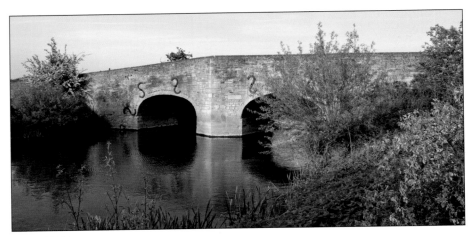

Ickford Bridge

Little Chalfont Nature Park

Little Chalfont – kestrel

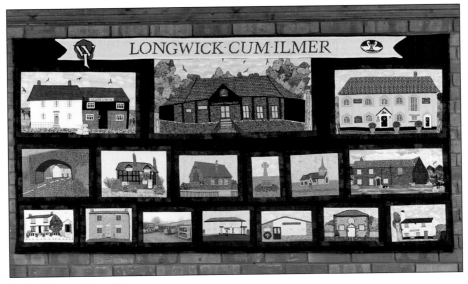

Longwick cum Ilmer Banner

Marlow on Thames

Olney Bend in the River Ouse

Olney Market Place

Penn and Tylers Green Woods

Princes Risborough Market Square

St Mary's Church, Radnage

Sands – Bluebell Sands

The Carpenters Arms, Slapton

Memorial Gardens, Stoke Poges

Stony Stratford

Wendover from Haddington Hill

Turville

Winslow Fatstock Show

🍁 HAZLEMERE

Hazlemere, situated on the outskirts of High Wycombe, could once have been called Hazlemoor as this name appears on old photographs on the wall of the post office.

Deadman Dane Bottom was the name given to a deep ravine in Hazlemere running at right angles to the high road from High Wycombe to Amersham and now known as Eastern Dene. It was part of wild moorland called Wycombe Heath.

There were very few houses in Hazlemere before the First World War. Scientist, Sir William Ramsay, lived at Beechcroft on the main road. He won the Nobel Prize for Chemistry in 1904 and was the discoverer of argon and the inert gaseous elements in air. Later Beechcroft's name was changed to Tylers Wood and became a Royal Grammar School boarding house.

The Misses Carter, two ladies from High Wycombe, concerned about the children in the area, founded a school somewhere between 1835-1840. This is thought to have been a 'dame school' in a building near Giles Farm, now part of a huge housing estate. A few years later in 1845, largely through their energy and determination, they had a church built in the area and dedicated it to the Holy Trinity.

In 1847 Hazlemere Church School was built and for over 100 years was the only school in the district. Pupils came from near and far. In the old log book 1900–1910 it is recorded that fees for pupils at the school went up from one penny to tuppence a week. Work was disrupted by parents who came to the school to protest that they could not afford the extra penny. The headmistress had to send for the vicar to reason with the parents.

Since the Second World War Hazlemere has grown very quickly. There are now big private housing estates, many shops and an 18-hole golf course in the area.

🍁 HEDGERLEY

Hedgerley village sits quietly in a narrow undulating valley within a few miles of the M4 and M40 motorways. The name Hedgerley comes from the Old English meaning 'Hycga's woodland clearing'. There are still working farms and extensive woodland in the area, some of which belongs to Eton College. Records of 1536 show that Eton 'boys were away at Heggeley on account of the plague at Eton'.

Entering the village, 20th-century development blends well into the woodland landscape. The large village green, village shop and post office are at the hub and there is still a local bus service.

Driving down the hill under the canopy of trees – magnificent on autumn days – we reach the village Conservation Area. With its picturesque pond, the White Horse pub dating back to 1685, Old Quaker House, Old School House, 19th-century church and a wealth of character properties, it is a step back in time. Take the footpath to Church Wood leading to open fields, home to cattle, muntjac and roe deer. The adjacent 35-acre RSPB Church Wood Nature Reserve attracts many birds, including woodpeckers, blackcaps and chiffchaffs. In spring, the bluebells, with their delicate scent, carpet the reserve's sunlit woodland glades.

The Old Quaker House is the most impressive historic house in Hedgerley. Based on information from the Weald & Downland Living Museum, the single storey wing on the right, dates from about 1400. Timber-framed with plaster noggin, it is split into two bays, each about 15 feet square. One bay was the living room, the other was for storage and sleeping. Roof timbers are heavily blackened by smoke from the

Hedgerley

central hearth escaping through a smoke hole. Such medieval buildings were always built end-on to the road, to make maximum use of the frontage.

In 2009, dendrochronological analysis of the main trusses of the large two-storey wing facing Village Lane, showed they came from trees felled in spring 1481 and spring and winter 1486/7. This dates the completion of the house to the end of the 15th century. Its timber-framed upper floor and attic overhang the ground floor. The side is brick and the original old tiled roof incorporated a smoke hole. Brick chimneys were installed in both wings and a red brick front garden wall with flint panels was added in the 18th century. The Hedgerley brick industry had thrived since 1344.

In 1650 the Old Quaker House became a Friends' Meeting House. A monthly Friends' Meeting was being held at the house by Quaker, George Salter, on 13 March 1666. There were about 60 Quakers present. During the meeting, the door flew open and a cloaked man strode in, crying 'make way there'. Producing a large stick from under his cloak, he struck a woman who had been too terrified to move. The Quakers were rounded up and their names taken for future punishment. This man was Ambrose Bennett, Justice of the Peace, described as 'overzealous' in his persecution of those he saw as disloyal to King Charles II (1630-1685), including the Quakers. On marriage, Bennett had acquired the Hedgerley Bulstrode estate, barely a mile from the Old Quaker House, so found out about the meeting.

The same Ambrose Bennett, with a group of roughnecks, drew his sword and attacked a Quaker funeral procession in 1665 on its way to the Friends' Meadow burial ground, Amersham. Greatly distressing the mourners, Bennett thrust the coffin from the bearers' shoulders to the ground and ordered that it be left on the highway. At night he had it removed to an unconsecrated burial site. The Quakers were arrested and imprisoned, without trial. In 1673, Bennett, due to his greed and extravagance, was sued for significant debt. The courts he had so often misused against others went against him. He fled to Virginia, only to find his settler friends there had been converted to Quakerism! He died shortly afterwards.

Villagers take great pride in their environment, gaining Buck's Best Kept Village status frequently since the 1980s. A Conservation Volunteers Group has been active for over 30 years, recently clearing the invasive holly in Kemsley Wood and restoring Church Meadow to a wild flower meadow. Nearby the Glebe Field now contains a maturing Community Orchard which hosts a Wassailing Ceremony each January. Hedgerley Scouts helped restore ponds in Church Meadow and Glebe Field. Their Christmas parties with entertainment for 'seniors' are very popular.

The three villages of Farnham Common, Farnham Royal and Hedgerley are a community and their churches form a United Benefice. Each September the Farnhams and Hedgerley Horticultural Show (founded 1975) guarantees friendly rivalry in all classes of exhibit. Since 2011 Farnham Common Community Library, run by unpaid volunteers, has provided library services, children's activities, IT support clinics, free PC access and a programme of popular outings for the villages.

The *Village Hedgerley* magazine reflects the vibrancy of village life. Our Memorial Hall is busy with Keep Fit, U3A, War Games, Film Clubs, WI and the popular Hedgerley Historical Society (HHS) formed in 1976. HHS marked the Millennium by producing a pictorial Parish Map of favourite buildings, wildlife, scenery and cartography of the village. As part of the First World War commemorations they produced a book on the *Ten Hedgerley Men From The Great War* who gave their lives in the conflict. The Memorial Hall was built in 1921 on land donated by Lord Burnham, as a lasting memorial to these and the other 78 men from the village who fought for their country. Ethel, the eldest daughter of Major C H Stevenson, of Hedgerley Park, who was killed in action in 1915, became the founding President of Hedgerley WI in 1921, which still thrives today.

On the horizon, residents are keenly aware of the proposed gravel extraction at Slade Farm at the edge of the village. Beaconsfield Motorway Services may raise issues in the future, although its distance and screening from the village has worked well so far.

While benefitting from its strategic location for transport and employment, Hedgerley remains an oasis in a busy world which is very much enjoyed by the residents, ramblers and visitors alike.

🍁 HIGH WYCOMBE

Nestled in the rolling countryside of the Chiltern Hills, High Wycombe is a market town midway between Oxford and London. Once the centre of the UK's furniture industry, highly skilled wood turners worked in the beech woods, turning chair legs and other cylindrical parts of chairs. Sadly, the industry has declined but Wycombe Museum, situated in an 18th-century building on a medieval site, houses an exhibition on the tools used relating to the furniture industry along with examples of the Windsor chair and other furniture.

Wycombe has a Georgian high street and if you look up at the buildings some of the architecture is fascinating. There is a red lion on a portico of a building that originally was the Red Lion Hotel. It is reported that both Winston Churchill and Benjamin Disraeli made election speeches standing on the portico next to the red lion. This building was demolished and replaced along with a new portico and red lion.

The Little Market House or Pepper Pot as it is known locally was designed by Robert Adam. There is also an arcaded Guild Hall. The market is held every Tuesday, Friday and Saturday.

The 12th-century parish church, All Saints, in the centre of the town, is said to be the largest in the county.

High Wycombe has a ceremony each year when the existing and new mayor are 'tolled out' and 'weighed in' to see if they are getting fat at the rate payers' expense. This is the only ceremony of its kind in the whole world. Although the mayor's weight is never revealed, the loss or gain is. If a gain, the words 'and some more' are spoken whereby there are lots of boos and jeers. Historically this would have been accompanied by thrown tomatoes and rotten fruit.

To the east of the town is The Rye and Holywell Mead. The park covers an area of more than 53 acres and has two children's playgrounds, football pitches and the Wycombe Rye Lido. The lido, with a gym and tennis courts, is well used by the community. The park includes areas formally known as Rye Mead, on which historically the people of High Wycombe had the right to pasture their cattle. Here is also the site of a Roman Villa and former watercress beds. The Dyke on the Rye is a large stretch of water that spills over a waterfall and into a stream that flows out of the park towards the east. It has a boating lake which is very popular in the summer months.

At the west end of the Rye is Pann Mill. It is the last operating watermill on the Wye, a tributary of the Thames. There have been watermills on this site since 1086. The remains of the mill were mostly demolished in 1971, however the remains were saved and a restoration project started which is ongoing. The mill holds open days at various times throughout the year.

High Wycombe has its own radio station *Wycombe Sound*, football team Wycombe Wanderers and brewery called Fishers. There is also a theatre, Wycombe Swan, a thriving WI called Wycombe Wenches, and Booker, the airfield. There are also many other community groups helping and involving residents from all walks of life. There are many wonderful local walks in the Chiltern countryside with the red kites soaring overhead and a number of famous residents including Disraeli, the Prime Minister who lived at Hughenden Manor, the actor and comedian, James Corden, and Howard Jones along with many more. All this makes High Wycombe an interesting place to live.

HOLMER GREEN

Holmer Green is a busy and thriving village with over 4000 inhabitants, surrounded by Metropolitan Green Belt and woodland. Appearing in the Domesday survey, the village began its existence as a hamlet, consisting of scattered farms and heathland. The origin of the name is probably the Saxon 'Holeme', meaning Mere Hollow.

Housing developments in the 1960s and 1970s have expanded the village to the size it is today, with three schools, numerous meeting halls, churches serving different denominations, pubs, and a range of shops, facilities and takeaways to suit all requirements. The 800th anniversary in 2008 was celebrated by planting eight cherry trees along Earl Howe Road.

In the 1800s, various local industries sprang up, using the surrounding beech woodland. A tennis racquet factory provided employment, and bodgers would dig their sawpits in the local woods to make chair parts for furniture makers in nearby High Wycombe. Cottage crafts occupied the womenfolk, particularly tambour beading, which was skilled work, and was famously used to decorate the gowns of well-known actresses and even a royal bride.

From the 1850s to 1950s, large areas of the village were planted with cherry orchards, and the popping and banging of devices used to scare the birds away would be a familiar sound in the summer months. One cherry picker was accidentally shot because the bird scarer, a young lad with a loaded gun, thought he was a bird.

Many road names feature references to orchards and cherries, while other local names refer to 19th-century poet Christina Rossetti and her brother Dante Gabriel Rossetti, who was also a poet and co-founder of the Pre-Raphaelite Brotherhood of artists. They would frequently visit their grandfather Gaetano Polidori at his house in what is now called Polidoris Lane.

Similarly, Clementi Avenue is named after Sir Cecil Clementi, a British colonial administrator who served as Governor of Hong Kong. His daughter, Dione Clementi, spent her wartime career in the Government Code and Cypher School at Bletchley.

A sprinkling of modern celebrities including TV star James Corden, professional footballer Bobby Barnes and actor Aaron Taylor-Johnson are all Holmer Green Senior School alumni.

The Common was formed in 1854 as a result of the Enclosure Act. Originally intended for sheep grazing and recreation, it was later donated to the Parish Council for public use. Older inhabitants used to speak of Old Natty's Ghost, who would walk from the Rookery across the Common on misty nights.

Nowadays, the village hosts a bi-annual visiting funfair and over the years it has been the obvious place to hold village fetes and more recently a music festival organised by the Holmer Green Village Society. The Common is well used as a general sports field and playground with swings and slides, and is popular for picnics and exercising dogs. Walkers and their canine companions also enjoy a network of footpaths in the beech woods surrounding the village, especially in the spring with their carpet of bluebells.

The Village Centre is the venue for clubs and societies such as the WI and Chadwick Ladies to meet, the Holmer Green Players to stage their performances, and the Village Produce Association to hold their Spring and Autumn Shows of homegrown fruit, vegetables, flowers and home baking.

Football and cricket have long sporting traditions in the village. The Cricket Club was founded in 1922 with matches played on the Common before retiring to The Bat & Ball pub for refreshment. At one time the pub sign for The Bat & Ball was changed to depict the bat as an animal, and the ball as the famous Golden Ball in West Wycombe. This caused such an outcry that it was quickly changed back to the original sign of cricket bat and ball. Local historian Stuart King tells the tale of the Holmer Green batsman whose wooden leg got broken after he was bowled out LBW! Nowadays, the cricket and football teams both achieve considerable success with wins in their respective leagues.

One of the main focal points of the village is the crossroads, with the village pond at one corner. Believed to be medieval in origin, the pond was the chief watering place for villagers to bring their animals to drink, with no ducks allowed, as they would foul the water. With no natural streams, water was also obtained from dew ponds and rainwater. In the past, the roof of local baker Freddie Tucker naturally attracted pigeons and their droppings. Like many other villagers, he collected rainwater running off his roof into a tank, presumably giving his bread its own unique flavour.

In the past, it has been said that people never want to move from Holmer Green once they've found it, and that sentiment still holds true today. The village is a much loved place for people of all ages to make their home, to work and to socialise, with its variety of amenities and welcoming community spirit. In spite of all its growth and development over the years, Holmer Green remains a village at heart.

🍁 HUGHENDEN

Hughenden has become very well-known because Benjamin Disraeli, Earl of Beaconsfield, lived at Hughenden Manor from 1847 until his death in 1881. Queen Victoria sent primroses, his favourite flower, to his funeral and these were placed on his grave in Hughenden churchyard, which is visited annually by the Primrose League.

The name Hughenden is derived from Hughendene or Hitchenden signifying the dene or valley of the Hitchen. The Manor, not far from the church, is now National Trust property and open to visitors most of the year. There are rooms exactly as they were in Disraeli's time and many mementoes of the great man.

St Michael and All Angels, 'the Church in the Park', must be situated in one of the prettiest sites in the country, with Hughenden Park on one side and farmland on the other. There has been a church there for over 800 years. Those with Second World War memories can recall the stained-glass east window being shattered by a flying bomb and then delicately being put together again using most of the old glass. There is a unique memorial to Disraeli in the church from Queen Victoria reading 'This memorial is placed by his grateful Sovereign and Friend Victoria R.I. Kings love him that speaketh right. Proverbs XVI 13'.

The Church House in the south-west corner of the churchyard is a medieval building which housed a small community of monks. It was restored in 1930 by Coningsby Disraeli and contains a minstrels' gallery.

Hughenden gradually developed from the church northwards with a farm, cottages and now estates on what used to be extensive orchards, mainly cherry. There are still some of the original old orchards left in gardens. A delightful stream meanders by the farm and under a pretty bridge, flowing and broadening into the Wye in Wycombe. Springs were very prevalent in the valley, causing some flooding, but these have now subsided, helped by a modern pumping station, from which half a million gallons of water are pumped daily from a 200 ft well.

Further on from the farm along the busy highway the mainly residential area is reached, with pleasant houses and gardens. A good proportion of young people with families live here and also retired folk. Many commute daily to their place of business in London and nearby towns.

Hughenden valley is a beautiful place, and, as most people say – 'we wouldn't want to live anywhere else'.

🍁 HYDE HEATH

'I would NEVER move away from Hyde Heath!' my neighbour was heard to say after local friends rallied round to help her following a traumatic event. It is this community spirit that makes Hyde Heath so special.

A 'hyde' is around 'a hundred acres of land, sufficient to support a family' so presumably the village name derives from a plot of one hundred acres of heathland.

The Village Hall was built in 1924, following the Great War, as a centre for village life. Today, 100 years on, activities include tap dancing, line dancing, parties and excellent shows from the Hyde Heath Theatre Club.

For the last 34 years, an Olde Tyme Music Hall show has been staged in the hall every November. Tickets are snapped up and the proceeds are divided between the hall, the Pre-School Group, the Scouts and the Infant School.

The Village Hall Committee works tirelessly to keep the hall viable and maintained – and organises the Village Fete.

The annual fete gets more popular as the years roll on. Many years ago, it was held in a field belonging to Mr Franklin, who ran the local coalyard. When the cricket field was laid out, it transferred to the common, where it grows each year. Now we have a vintage aeroplane flypast, and classic car display. Eric Coates, who wrote the Dam Busters March, came to live in the village for a short while in 1943 to escape war-torn London, but only stayed long enough to write his Four Centuries Suite before returning to London.

Murder came to Hyde Heath in 1966, when the local lay preacher's wife, Dr Helen Davison, was found in Hodgemoor Wood with her Jack Russell staying faithfully beside her body. No one has been brought to account for the crime, although rumours were rife at the time.

The Village Society, first formed in 1965, comes together to fight local causes such as the HS2 project.

For many years, *Olde Tyme Music Hall* has been staged in the village hall, in November. Tickets are usually snapped up and the proceeds are divided between the Village Hall, the Pre-School Group, the Scouts and the Infants School. The group, organised by Terry Cann, has made well over £60,000 over the years. Hyde Heath Theatre Club also put on performances of an excellent standard several times a year.

A Millennium embroidery hangs in the village hall, executed by many of our WI members and co-ordinated by Ann Stevens, a founder member of Hyde Heath Evening WI. She was an enthusiastic villager who worked tirelessly for the village over many years.

The school was built at the turn of the 20th century and was enlarged in around 1970 to accommodate two more classrooms. It has an outstanding OFSTED report.

The flagpole on the common flies the union flag on national occasions. More recently, one can request the flag to be raised on birthdays – for a small fee.

St Andrew's Church was renovated through bequests and new stained-glass windows are dedicated to the memory of the local couple who made it possible, and who also paid for improvements to the village shop. Like Hyde Heath Chapel, regular Sunday services are held in the church each week. The chapel hosts a meal for retired villagers once a month and it is well attended.

A Handbell Group meet in the church on alternate Fridays – they welcome villagers and enthusiasts from further afield. At Christmas, they can be heard playing carols in The Plough pub.

A themed village meal was inaugurated here a few years ago, which provides a very pleasant evening. The Plough is now the only pub in the village after the closure of The Red Cow, now a coal merchant's.

The village doubled in size in the 1960s, when a large development of houses was built on local farmland. This put new life into the village

Hyde Heath church

and many residents commute into London on the Metropolitan Line each day. However, plenty of villagers work in trades locally and they have been a huge boon to village life. You can get most jobs done with a quick phone call.

🍁 IBSTONE

The small village of Ibstone straddles a ridge of the Chiltern Hills approximately ten miles west of High Wycombe. Some village points afford magnificent views of the Hambleden Valley below. The origins of Ibstone go back before the Norman Conquest and the village was included in the Domesday Survey of 1086, at which time it was called Hibestanes.

Merton College, Oxford, has been associated with the village from 1270. In 1284 there were 26 tenant farmers and Ibstone remained a farming community until mains water and electricity came into the village in 1935. In 1852, the first of the present school buildings was erected. At that date, the village population was 310 with some 50 children at school. There were five farms, two pubs, a grocer, post office, a wheelwright and a blacksmith. The village was a thriving self-supporting community.

There has been a church in Ibstone for over 1,000 years. The present building dates from about 1200 and has many interesting features including one of the oldest wooden pulpits in England. Like many villages, Ibstone has a windmill, originally built in the 16th century, Cobstone Mill. The present building dates from around 1816 and is an unusual 12-sided smock mill. This mill has featured in many films and TV shows but will principally be remembered as the family home in *Chitty Chitty Bang Bang*.

John Wesley recorded that he preached at Ibstone on two separate occasions in 1767 and 1769. It was not until 1862 that a Methodist Chapel was established which continued to be used as a religious meeting place for approximately 100 years. Local legend has it that an attempt was made to build another church on a new site in Grays Lane, but the Devil objected to a church being built on his property so the rising structure repeatedly fell giving that particular spot its present name of Hell Corner.

The village has held a firework display and bonfire on the Common on November 5th since the early 1970s. Soup and sausages help to keep out the cold. One of the major events in Ibstone's calendar is the village show and fete which is organised by the local Horticultural Society and is held on the Common in August. This is a very popular event which attracts many people from South Bucks. Any profit is donated to local charities.

🍁 ICKFORD

Surrounded by wonderful countryside, Ickford has a beautiful 12th-century church and an excellent village primary school. Now an academy, it may be small but every child is taught to play a musical instrument and speak a foreign language. The school plays a large part in the community, with pupils involved in many village activities and locals able to play badminton in the school sports hall.

The village shop and post office is proudly owned by the villagers. Years ago, local residents took shares in the shop to avoid losing it and, as stakeholders, they now ensure it stays viable and well used.

Every year, there is a tug of war over the River Thame which separates Buckinghamshire and Oxfordshire. Tiddington field a team to represent Oxfordshire and Ickford hold their own on the Bucks side. This fun tradition started in 1953, to mark the Queen's coronation, and has taken place every year since. A male and female team compete and usually both sides end up in the river. It is a highlight of the village's social calendar and is well attended by both sets of villagers.

There is now just one village pub, The Rising Sun, with a magnificent thatched roof. The pub is well used by villagers as a meeting place, as is the village hall, which was built by the villagers themselves.

Ickford is still a very small village and many of the residents have lived here for more than 30 years. Not many houses come up for sale and those that do are usually snapped up by parents wanting to get their children into our excellent school.

🍁 IVINGHOE

Ivinghoe sits beside the Chiltern Hills, with Ivinghoe Beacon, site of an ancient hillfort to the east and beautiful views over the Vale of Aylesbury to the west. It lies at the point where Upper and Lower Icknield Way meet, part of one of the oldest trackways in the country. Ivinghoe Beacon is situated at the start of the Ridgeway trail and the village has many visitors in the summer. Cyclists abound on the roads surrounding the village, keen to test themselves on the challenging hills. There is a thriving campsite at Town Farm, Ivinghoe where campers can wake to the splendid view of the Beacon.

In the centre of Ivinghoe village stands the handsome old brewery house, which was home to the family who ran the brewery. The brewery started in 1720 and dominated the village for 200 years, employing the men in the village unless they were agricultural labourers. The Brewery

House became Ivinghoe Youth Hostel and is now a family home once again; it looks to the west over the green, known as 'the lawn', towards a farm and a working watermill.

On one side of the lawn is the King's Head Restaurant, famous for its Aylesbury Duck and a hostelry of some sort for hundreds of years. On the other side is the old Village School, now a Community Centre with an award-winning café. Next to the Brewery House is the 16th-century Town Hall, and the old market place where the straw plaiters used to sell their plaits, now a community library and post office. Next door is a hairdresser and a chemist. On the other side of the Brewery House and by the bus shelter against the church wall is a long hook for pulling thatch off burning buildings, and a mantrap for catching poachers.

The large 13th-century church has wooden angels in the roof and interesting poppy heads on the pew ends. Particularly interesting is the carved mermaid. The church bells ring in the tower and there is a thriving team of handbell ringers.

Further up the road are the allotments – once a group of dwellings were sited here where locals would plait the straw, but these were later sold.

The last working pub in the village is The Rose and Crown, where Lord Bernard Miles entertained drinkers with songs about the village and villagers. He was an actor and he opened the Mermaid Theatre in London in 1959, the first new one to be opened there since the 17th century. He was made a life peer in 1969 for his services to the theatre. A star of many films, he was known for his comic monologues mostly about villagers from Ivinghoe and the surrounding area and written in the local dialect.

A new primary school was built in 1967 between the two villages of Ivinghoe and Pitstone. Brookmead School and Windmill Pre-School are situated beside Whistlebrook stream on the boundary of the two villages. Both villages come together at the annual church fete with floats, stalls and, finally, a well-fought tug of war.

🍁 THE KIMBLES

The Kimbles are made up of Great Kimble and Little Kimble. According to local tradition, Kimble is named after Cunobelin (in Shakespeare's play he is Cymbeline). Due to famine in 1315, the hamlet of Little

Kimble failed. In 1885, the two parishes were merged and now also contain the hamlets of Kimblewick and Marsh. The Kimbles lie to the south of Aylesbury (5 miles) and the ancient routes of the Ridgeway and Icknield Way passed through this rural parish. There are many walks on public footpaths following the 40 miles of the Aylesbury Ring routes.

The original hamlet of Great Kimble was situated next to St Nicholas' church before its demise following the Black Death. In 1635, MP John Hampden, also a church warden at St. Nicholas', refused to pay 'ship money', which began a chain of events that resulted in the execution of Charles I. All Saints' Church, Little Kimble, is on the Ellesborough/Wendover Road and wall paintings have been uncovered from the 14th century and there are some remnants of early stained glass. Kimble Free Church is situated in Grove Lane (known locally as the Church by the Bridge) and supports the village community with various charity fundraising events. Twice a year, the Ellesborough Silver Band leads the hymns at Christmas and once again in the summer.

The Swan, said to be haunted by a former landlady, is a local favourite with a recently refurbished children's play area.

The Stewart Hall, named after patron Charles Edward Stewart of Ladymede House, thrives in Little Kimble. Opened on Armistice Day 1925, the hall is used by the community for the Parish Council, Kimble and Ellesborough WI, the Horticultural Society, village flower shows, Pilates, dog training, theatre club and the local Lodge.

There is a small railway station on the Princes Risborough/Aylesbury Road in Little Kimble and trains run to Aylesbury and Princes Risborough and to Marylebone. There is also a frequent bus service to Princes Risborough and Aylesbury.

The village is very fortunate as it has its own school whose pupils attend a church service once a month along with parents and have weekly visits to their ecology site at Smokey Row with a classroom for outdoor studies and activities. Great Kimble School began as a Sunday School in St Nicholas' Church in 1805. The original village school house from 1832 had girls learning their lacemaking upstairs while the boys learned to read and write – the girls just to read. Another junior school, Ladymede House, was a private school where several celebrities were educated. It was eventually closed to be reborn as Griffin House School.

The area around the Kimbles is a close-knit farming community and every Easter a point-to-point is held at Kimblewick which is very well attended and there is also the Kimblewick Hunt Kennels. Although the Chequers Estate is in the Ellesborough Parish, many of the estate workers lived in the Kimbles.

LACEY GREEN & LOOSLEY ROW

Our twin villages are on the escarpment of the Chiltern Hills, the highest point in Buckinghamshire. Some areas are over 700ft high, which gives us wonderful views over the Vale of Aylesbury and beyond, but also accounts for the cold, breezy, and sometimes misty weather that we enjoy.

This is a very vibrant community and we are fortunate to have a very good C of E junior school which is often oversubscribed as children come from surrounding areas. The school is directly opposite St John's Church, for which we have a vicar living nearby.

Our Village Hall is very well used for a variety of activities, and also houses a local shop run on a voluntary basis. This was built for the Millennium year and stalwarts from the villages were active in obtaining grants and funds to make this happen!

We have three village pubs, which are all thriving and help to strengthen the community spirit.

The Sports Club takes part in football and cricket matches and has a pavilion which, in addition to social events, houses the nursery school. Adjacent to the sports field are a children's playground and tennis courts. The Tennis Club has been revived in recent years and now attracts adults and children alike.

Our most renowned feature is the windmill, which contains mid-17th-century machinery, and is probably the oldest of its type in the country. It last worked in 1915, and was restored from the point of collapse by local volunteers over about twenty years starting in the early 1970s. The mill opens every Sunday afternoon from Easter to the end of September.

Farming activities are very much in evidence with a dairy farm in the centre of the village. Beef cattle are also raised and sold locally and crops are grown including wheat, oilseed rape and maize.

🍁 LANE END

The village of Lane End sits high in the Chilterns and was well known locally in recent years for having five pubs and two duck ponds. Whilst the ducks still swim happily on the ponds there is now only one pub and an Indian restaurant.

The once busy woodyard, supplying the furniture trade, is now a small industrial estate and the furniture factories have made way for new houses and Gracewell Care Home. Many new faces have been welcomed into the village with the advent of all the new houses that have been built around, especially on the former Elga site, and a lot of the new residents have joined in with various village activities.

There is a thriving Village Hall where Lane End Players put on some excellent productions and the organisations that meet there include the Bridge Club, Four Ends Flower Club, and The Evening Women's Institute. The WI presented the clock that now adorns the front of the Memorial Porch to celebrate 100 years of the Women's Institute in England and Wales. The front porch of the hall contains the War Memorial honouring Lane End's war dead but in 1999 a new memorial was erected on the green opposite which not only includes the names of those who lost their lives from Lane End but also the seven Canadians whose plane crashed in Widdenton Woods nearby, on their way back from a bombing raid in April 1945.

The new Community Centre, adjacent to Lane End Primary School, is also well supported by a lunch club, coffee shop, Over 50s Exercise Group, Youth Club, the Lane End Older Persons' Action Group and many more.

Lane End is very fortunate with the amenities in the village. When the post office was due to close there was great concern but luckily this was taken on by the Londis supermarket. There used to be two butchers' shops and when the second one closed the Lacey family, who have farmed the area for seven generations, at Bolter End Farm, decided it was a good opportunity to open a Farm Shop and to include a butcher, selling locally produced meat. The milk they supply is from their own Guernsey herd, which you can see grazing in fields nearby. The shop is a great success.

After 200 years of Methodism in Lane End the congregation of the Methodist Chapel found that the building was becoming too expensive to repair, especially with a smaller number of people trying to fundraise.

It was finally sold in 2008 and the members were invited to hold their services in Holy Trinity, the Parish Church of Lane End. This proved very successful until 2017 when the congregation joined the Avenue Methodist Church in High Wycombe.

There is an active Conservation Group and the members help to keep the footpaths clear and carry out valuable work in improving the environment. There are any number of footpaths for those who like walking and many rambling groups can be found exploring the beautiful countryside and beech woods. In the summer, there is an abundance of wild orchids on Moor Common and you may be lucky enough to spot a Purple Emperor butterfly amongst the trees there.

LITTLE CHALFONT

Little Chalfont was created in the 20th century with the arrival of the Metropolitan Railway – before that it had farms and cottages spread through the area but no specific name. When the railway arrived in 1915, it created a station called Chalfont and Latimer. Up until then the road through had been called Chalfont Road. In 1925, the Chalfont St Giles Parish Council had referred to the village as Little Chalfont, and in 2007 it gained its own parish council status. In 2017, Little Chalfont had 6,858 residents.

The village inhabitants have a varied living with a large proportion commuting into London on the Metropolitan Line and overground Chiltern Line and then in the other direction on the Chiltern Line to Aylesbury.

During the Second World War, Bertram Mills Circus was evacuated to Little Chalfont as the widow of Bertram Mills lived at Pollards Wood House where there was land and stabling. Members remember hearing elephants trumpeting loudly over a wide area. Dorothy Paget, the famous but reclusive race horse trainer, also lived nearby. One of the founder members of the local WI was a keen swimmer and was responsible for starting the Swimming Club and helping to build Amersham Pool.

The village was once dominated by GE Healthcare but they have now scaled their business back in the village, but are still a large local employer. Little Chalfont has four schools, three churches and boasts a good variety of coffee houses, cafés and restaurants. It has a butcher, two bakeries, florist, village store, dry cleaner and who could ignore the craft beer shop? It has three dentists, a doctors' surgery, pharmacy, chiropodist and opticians. Hairdressers and beauty salons can also be found in the parade of shops. Many of the family businesses have been replaced by well-known High Street names but the butchers, Robertsons, opened in the early 1960s remains in the hands of the original owner's son. The shops are separated by the village triangle, a garden maintained by the village WI that has many displays throughout the year.

On the second Saturday of the month in the Village Hall, there is a thriving Farmers' Market and Craft Market, where the local WI provide tea and cake and the local men-in-sheds sell their very unusual gifts. There are lots of local groups that use the Village Hall including a toddler group, U3A, Bumps & Babies, Good Companions and two WI groups.

The village has a community library which not only has many books, DVDs and magazines to borrow but also has film nights which are very well attended.

Annually, we have a village day where all the local clubs, schools, shops and businesses join in with a cornucopia of events from a fun run and dog show to a scarecrow competition and bake off. With charity and food stalls, it is truly a family event.

The jewel in our crown has to be our Nature Park which was opened in 2016 and boasts rare grassland, a wild flower meadow and semi-natural woodland. Open to all from dawn to dusk, it is used by schools and local clubs to discover nature and the villagers use it for picnics or just a lovely amble.

Westwood Park is a great open space which has a children's park, a cricket pavilion with cricket pitch in the summer and then football pitches in the winter. It also has tennis courts and an all-sport court which of course gets very busy when Wimbledon is on, as do the local tennis club courts. The park borders a large wood that leads down to the Chess Valley.

One of the oldest buildings in the village is Beel House, a Grade II listed 16th-century house originally owned by the Duke of Buckingham. Since then, actor Dirk Bogarde, pop star Ozzy Osbourne and TV host Robert Kilroy Silk have all lived in the house. The village has had a host of other celebrities living in the village too, including pop star Noel Gallagher and footballer David Platt.

All in all Little Chalfont is a thriving village but, as with many other places, it is overcome by the volume of traffic passing through and the inevitable parking problems. However, there are many loyal local people who are determined to keep the life of the village as vibrant and friendly as possible and we owe them a great debt of gratitude.

🍁 LITTLE KINGSHILL

Little Kingshill is a small village in the parish of Little Missenden. The origins of the village appear to date back to around AD 900 when a monastery was founded where Ashwell Farm now stands. William the Conqueror gave a manor and lands to the Earl of Aufrics, now known as Affricks. Ashwell and Affricks Farm still exist. After the Earl's death, the land reverted back to the crown. The hamlet name 'Kingshill' means a hill in possession of the King, which folklore suggests was King John. The oldest building in the village is believed to be the farmhouse at Ashwell Farm, and it is claimed that a monk's lodge at the farm – 'Kyngeshull' or Kingshall – was used by the king en route to Windsor. King John granted the manor to Hugh de Gournay in 1213. The addition of 'Little' is believed to have been added to the hamlet to distinguish it from the village of Great Kingshill. Around 1291, Affricks Farm was given to Godstow nunnery.

Very little seems to have been recorded between 1200 and 1800. In 1660, Boot Farm was built and the occupant was the bailiff in charge of the cherry orchards for which the village was famous. In 1814, the Baptist church was founded, and the church built in 1834. Until that time, folk from the village would have walked to the Little Missenden Parish Church of St John founded in 975. It is also believed that King John had visited Little Missenden, a house on the edge of the village being named Kingshall.

During the latter part of the 19th century, the village began to develop. There were three public houses, the first school commenced, the cricket club was formed and housing increased. Men who worked on the construction of the new railway line lodged in the village. Residents were mainly farm workers, chair makers, drovers and lace makers. In 1841, there were 38 houses with a population of 186. As housing and the population increased, local workers included accountants, antique furniture dealers, chauffeurs, children's maids and braidworkers. In 1925, tambour beading was also done and it is reported that Shirley Bassey's dresses were made in the village.

The village lost eleven men during the First World War and Mrs Pilley, who started the WI here, was instrumental in setting up the Memorial and

Thanksgiving Fund. On the common, eleven trees were planted in their memory, and are maintained to this day. A further five names were added after the Second World War.

An arboretum was started in 1917 by one Thomas Priest. By the time he died in 1942, he had planted some 400 trees, mainly conifers. Friends of the Arboretum were formed in 1983, the Arboretum opened to visitors the following year and it still has several open days throughout the year. In 1925, New Road was built – the second road in the village. Brownies arrived in 1938 but Scouts did not follow until the 1970s. In the 1930s the village had a post office and a general store. A new village hall and school were built in 1956. In 1962, a village society was formed with a membership of just 30 but this has grown to over 400 members. Today the village has a combined primary and nursery school for children from 3-11 years old, a village hall, a Baptist Church, a church hall and one pub.

LITTLE MARLOW & WELL END

Little Marlow and Well End are the two biggest settlements in the civil parish of Little Marlow. They grew up originally around the church and the abbey respectively. Now Little Marlow is a small village off the A4155 in southern Buckinghamshire and Well End has been overtaken by the expansion of Bourne End.

At first sight, Little Marlow is unchanged from centuries ago with its church, manor house, timber-framed and red brick cottages and the King's Head and Queen's Head public houses. The village school is still functioning, albeit with children from further afield, and the recreation ground and pavilion, given to the village by the then-lady of the manor 100 years ago as a war memorial, are the focus of many activities including the WI.

However, this is no longer a predominantly farming community. Much of the farmland has been dug for gravel, leaving lakes. Emmett's Farm to the north of the main road has diversified and provides the only village shop. As well as a fairly traditional farm shop there is a fish and meat shop, an antiques shop in a former threshing barn and the 'gun shop' – a country activities store.

The most famous lady of the manor in recent times was Melanie Brown of the Spice Girls, who lived there for a few years and was married in the church in a ceremony completely sealed off from the many visitors who descended on Little Marlow for the day. This was not entirely to the disadvantage of the village as enterprising car park charging helped provide some upgraded children's play equipment for the recreation ground!

The recreation ground is meticulously maintained by the cricket club groundsman and limes have replaced the elms that were the casualty of Dutch elm disease. The village presents an idyllic scene on a summer afternoon and a lovely backdrop for the annual village fete. The WI provides the cakes for the teas, and the stalls are the same from year to year. Everyone gets a chance to meet their friends and acquaintances, admire the dog with the waggiest tail and cheer on the children's sports and the inter-pub tug of war. A large amount of money is raised which is put back into the village amenities and charities.

The speed of vehicles on the main road has been a cause of concern from the earliest days of the Parish Council – in 1905 they were trying to get the 10 mph speed limit enforced. Now there is a good pavement, but a much higher speed limit, and the walk from Little Marlow to Well End is more pleasant beside the lake or along the banks of the River Thames. This leads to Coldmoorholm Lane where the wharf on the river bank was once a thriving transport hub where wheat, malt and wood were loaded for their journey to supply London. Spade Oak Farmhouse was a centre for hiring horses for hauling barges to Marlow. Rumour has it that the barge owners found the fees too high so they set up a ferry. This ran for foot passengers until the 1950s. Between the farm and the wharf is the railway line which was opened in 1873, thus starting the decline in the river trade and bringing development to Bourne End.

One of the developers was Robert Haben Tebb who bought the Abbey Farm, the site of the former Abbey, and started building the Abbotsbrook Estate to provide weekend homes for 'the elite of London Society' who could take advantage of the new trains. Unfortunately he became bankrupt in 1907 and the estate was sold.

The sale plan shows the estate divided into lots of small plots, but many of these were combined and iconic Edwardian houses built, connected by navigable streams as well as private roads. Wandering around today, you do get the feeling of stepping back in time. It has social gatherings among the residents including fireworks, a regatta around the pool followed by a barbecue, sports for the children and streamside festivities.

The design included a village hall which still provides a larger venue than the pavilion for community activities with a thriving pre-school, bridge club and Brownies regularly meeting there as well as private parties and the annual parish meeting.

Returning to the main road, we find a cluster of old houses and The Black Lion pub. The house and fields of Well End Farm are still there, but the barns and cowhouses have been converted to houses. The Old Malt House opposite is further evidence of the busy past of the hamlet, when barley was grown and made into malt for 'export' to London from Spade Oak Wharf.

Little Marlow is no longer self-sufficient but it is still a community that comes together for the important church services of Christmas, Easter, Harvest and Remembrance Sunday. The present owners of the Manor House are generous in their hospitality to the village and visitors from near and far are welcome to share the school, the recreation ground and pavilion, visit the pubs and farm shops or walk to the river and the surrounding countryside.

🍁 LITTLE MISSENDEN

Those who now live in this small, close-knit village and pride themselves on belonging to a caring community, would have been horrified to have heard themselves described as a 'Godless lot', as were the villagers of the 1800s, when a well-known revivalist cleric of the time was appointed by Earl Howe, the patron, to the living. Objecting to the inadequate size of the vicarage, Earl Howe allowed him to enlarge and alter it, which resulted in a bill for £1,500, a lot of money in those days. When Earl Howe was presented with the bill, this was his answer 'I told you you could alter the place, I didn't say I would pay for it'. The repayment of this sum went on until the year before the Rev. W. H. Davis came in the 1920s.

The wonderful old church of St John the Baptist, over 1,000 years old, owes much to the devoted love and service of its ministers.

The village school, once a large establishment, serving the families in Hyde Heath and Holmer Green, is now a very sought-after Infant School. We are lucky that the school staff encourage their pupils, who mostly live out of the village, to join in our activities.

A different kind of school was the one where the Chiltern Hospital stands. This was originally Little Missenden Abbey. There is reputed to be a secret passage between the Great and Little Abbeys, used during Henry VIII's Dissolution of the Monastries, but it has never been found. There is, however, a ghost at the Abbey. If you sleep in a certain room in the gatehouse on Twelfth Night, you will be aware of a presence, and experience the sensation of thumbscrews being painfully applied!

In the late 1930s, Little Missenden Abbey was a school for difficult children, with the emphasis on self expression and subsequently, it was hoped, self discipline. Boys from 7–11 years and girls from 12-19 boarded there, and it was run by Mrs Lister-Kay, a child psychologist and a friend of Eric Gill, whose studio at Speen was the venue for many young artists and musicians of the day. In fact for a while the composer Michael Tippett taught at the school, and Edmund Rubbra was a frequent visitor.

The inauguration of the Little Missenden Festival in 1960 was the brain child of Mrs Pat Harrison. Music concerts and lectures on art and literature take place each October.

Few visitors to the village fail to gaze with admiration at the Manor House. Seen through the wrought-iron gates are beautiful lawns and gardens. This wonderful old part-Tudor building has been the home of many interesting people, notably Lady Alice Ashley and Brigadier Roger Peake, both of whom gave dedicated service to the Royal Family.

Finally, to complete the picture of our village life, we must mention the Village Hall. Once an old First World War army hut, this centre of our village activities, through the work and dedication of village stalwarts is now a very presentable renovated building, in continual use. Little Missenden feels it has a right to be called a 'caring and close-knit community'.

🍁 LONG CRENDON

Long Crendon was originally called Creodun, a Saxon word meaning Creoda's Hill, Creoda being the son of Cedric, or Cerdic, the first king of the West Saxons. A large village two miles north of Thame, it came into prominence towards the end of the 16th century with its needlemaking industry. Lacemaking likewise was one of its crafts, having been brought into Buckinghamshire villages by foreign refugees as early as the 16th century. It provided work for a large proportion of the women and girls, some of them learning even from the age of five.

The village's long meandering main street, bounded at one end by the impressive 14th-century grey limestone church, and at the other end by the Churchill Arms, is picturesque with its colour-washed houses and cottages, mostly of the 17th century. Long Crendon's oldest inn, also in the main street, is the Eight Bells, situated towards the church end and close to the famous old Courthouse.

Long Crendon, in common with many another village, seems to have had its fair share of ghosts! There was the poltergeist believed to have haunted the Courthouse, the galloping horseman of Lower End, an unhappy little lady in much the same area whose soul is now said to be shut up in a salt box buried in a chimney wall at The Mound, and the inevitable woman in grey who is said to haunt the church. She, like the rest of them, is said to be 'friendly and harmless, and glides away to keep her secret'.

LONG MARSTON & PUTTENHAM

Long Marston grew up around a crossroads near the borders of Herts, Bucks and Beds. Anyone driving through the village past the old pub, the school, village hall and up the slight hill next to the church, would scarcely think that this peaceful place belied a gruesome past. For Long Marston was the scene of the last witch hunt in England.

It all began in 1746 when a local woman, Ruth Osbourne, begged some buttermilk from her neighbour John Butterfield. When he refused, Ruth cursed him and went on her way. However, five years later John had fallen on hard times and believed that Ruth's curse had been the cause of all his troubles. Ruth and her husband had become destitute and were living in the workhouse in Tring when John and another villager Thomas Colley decided that she and her husband should be tried as witches. Word got around the local towns, and a crowd of thousands descended on Tring, eventually managing to drag Ruth and her husband back to Long Marston. Here they both perished after being dragged mercilessly through the village pond. Thomas Colley even collected money from the crowd in exchange for this entertainment. Eventually, Colley was brought to justice and hanged at Gubblecote Cross, on the edge of the village.

Thankfully, as the years went by, life in Long Marston settled into a more civilised routine and by the end of the 1950s, the village had become quite self-sufficient, having a butcher's shop, a baker's, post office, sweetshop and hairdresser's. There was a blacksmith, carpenter, cobbler and chimney sweep. For entertainment, there were at one time four pubs, and weekly dances in the village hall. The school, which stood in the centre of the village, was a victim of a German bomb in 1941. All the children had gone home but tragically the headmistress was still in the building.

The Queens Head pub in Long Marston

A new school was built in 1951, and the population of Long Marston began to grow. We now have around 800 residents, but our amenities have disappeared over the years. The shops and small businesses have come and gone leaving only the Queen's Head pub standing at the crossroads as it has done since a hundred years before the witch hunt.

For anyone with time to spare we have a variety of activities in the village. There is a football club, cricket club and tennis club, who run fundraising quiz nights from time to time. We also have a Horticultural Society who organise the major events of the village such as the panto, the village show, firework night in November and the very popular carols around the Christmas tree with guest appearance by Santa and as much free mulled wine as you can drink! The school PTA also arranges quiz nights for the village and a summer barbeque for the pupils and their families. And of course we have our WI which provides refreshments at village events, and invites the village to enjoy our talks now and then.

The countryside around Long Marston is a paradise for dog owners with a wealth of footpaths criss-crossing the fields, making it possible to walk across the fields to nearby villages or the Grand Union Canal. We are lucky to have our unique Black Poplar Trail, which takes a route through the fields passing some of these rare trees which grow well in our low-lying landscape. Another popular walk passes over the scene of a horrific air crash which happened in 1945. A Liberator took off from the nearby American air base but in thick fog crashed through the treetops into the field where it burst into flames, killing three of the crew.

The Black Poplar Trail passes close to our Old Church Tower. Set amongst dark yew trees, this tower was once part of a Chapel of Ease, and dates back to the 12th century. Most of the church was demolished during the 1800s, and due to its fragile and dangerous state only the vicar and the bride and groom were allowed inside for the last wedding to take place there! In the early 2000s, the tower was restored thanks to a supreme effort by local residents. The total cost was £44,000, half of which was given by English Heritage, and the other half by holding cream tea afternoons, concerts and dinners over a number of years.

One disadvantage of the flat terrain, is the unfortunate side effect of flooding. We have many streams and ditches for drainage but occasionally over the years these have become overwhelmed during the wet months and caused devastation by flooding the village and severely damaging some of the houses.

Our WI sister-village Puttenham boasts a beautiful church dating back to the 13th century, and a very grand village hall, known as Cecilia Hall. Every year at 6am on May Day morning, a choir sings from the top of the church tower, watched by a cluster of early risers. After the singing, everyone adjourns into Cecilia Hall for a slap-up breakfast, and for those who don't have to go to work, a glass or two of fizz to welcome Spring.

In 2013, Puttenham was officially celebrated as a Thankful Village, which meant that all those who went away to fight in the First World War returned home safely. A special flag was made and flown from the church tower and a memorial stone waas erected on the roadside.

Although a tiny community, Puttenham is famous locally for its amazing jumble sales, harvest suppers and afternoon teas, with a dedicated team of helpers to make it all take place.

Indeed, the very essence of village life is being part of a small community where people are brought together by school, clubs, church, socialising at the pub, or even walking the dog. These things have not changed over the years, and we hope that they will continue to make our villages happy places for all those who live here in the future.

LONGWICK CUM ILMER

On the borders of Buckinghamshire and Oxfordshire, Longwick, as its name suggests, is a 'long village' consisting mainly of farmland.

Longwick was on a drovers' route from the Welsh Borders and Herefordshire to London. This meant cattle were driven through the village, which became a stopping point for both animals and drovers themselves.

Longwick originally had six ale houses and public houses catering for the drovers; cattle grazed in the nearby fields and drank from the ponds and streams. In the early 1900s, the Old Tree Pub opened in Walnut Tree Lane to cater for the workers building the railway line.

The hamlet of Ilmer, mentioned in the Domesday Book, had been the largest part of the parish until the Black Death wiped out the population in 1349. It is now an attractive place to live with a pretty church, the nave of which dates back to the 12th century, a pond and several listed buildings.

Horsenden, Owlswick and Meadle complete the parish. Horsenden was also mentioned in the Domesday Book and Meadle had strong associations with the Quakers. George Fox, founder of the Society of Friends (later to be called the Quakers), held his meetings there in the 1600s. Now in the 21st century, a Natural Burial Ground has been established in Meadle.

In 1795, William Walker left the employ of the Earl of Buckingham and moved to Longwick. A wheelwright's business was established, together with a blacksmith's and a sawmill. In the 1900s, the most imposing landmark in Longwick was the chimney at Walker's Sawmill, one of the largest sawmills in the country at that time. However, it was closed in the late 1960s, and an attractive housing estate was built on the land. Recently some nearby agricultural land has been sold for development, and old barns have been beautifully converted into sought-after homes. Longwick Mill, a listed building on the Icknield Way, closed in the late 1990s to be converted into private dwellings with more homes built on the adjacent yard land.

With the help of local people a book, *A History of Longwick-cum-Ilmer* was researched and published for the Millennium in 2001 containing a detailed account of how the village began. This account also included mention of the now infamous Acid House Party, which took place in 1989 and was reported in national newspapers.

A unique feature of Longwick is the May Day celebration of garlands dating back to at least 1850. Local gardeners grow Crown Imperials specifically to top the crowns and sceptres which are themselves covered in spring flowers. These colourful crowns and sceptres, made by the children, are then paraded through the village.

Longwick has a friendly, family-run post office and village shop and there is also a petrol station with a convenience store. The author Alison Uttley dedicated her 1963 book *Grey Rabbit's May Day* to the children of Longwick School, which became an Academy in 2018. There is a small business estate which includes among others, an upholsterer's and a cake decorating business, and nearby a garden machinery and fencing business as well as a plant nursery.

The Red Lion is the last remaining pub in the village. It is family-owned with a friendly atmosphere providing good food and overnight accommodation.

In the late 1980s a new Village Hall was built with all modern facilities and it now hosts a wide range of activities for all ages and tastes. By way of decoration, Longwick Evening WI installed a colourful wall hanging in the Hall, made by members, depicting interesting and distinctive buildings in the village.

There is a thriving Scout Group catering for boys and girls of all ages up to 17 years who meet in the Scout Headquarters, purpose built in the late 1970s.

The village benefits from a service provided by the Princes Risborough

Area Community Bus. The bus, run by volunteers, provides a Hail and Ride service to Princes Risborough four times a day during the week for those without transport, and for those who prefer to leave their cars at home.

🍁 MAIDS MORETON

Maids Moreton, originally Morton meaning 'marshy settlement', is one of the oldest villages in Buckinghamshire and situated just a mile from Buckingham. The name derives from two Pever sisters who lived at the Manor and who gave money for the building of the church in the 15th century. They are depicted in St Edmund's Church to this day. As with a lot of villages, life has changed and old customs and stories of local folk are not as prevalent as in the past. The village still has a friendly atmosphere, a thriving church, a village hall built in 1920, the thatched 17th-century Wheatsheaf pub together with two nursing homes.

An active Conservation Group exists in the village; they maintain the natural areas of the village and have created a wildlife area in Scotts Lane. An annual litter pick is held around the village. In 2014, the Group undertook an archaeological dig on The Mound behind what was the Buckingham Arms pub, now Meadow Bank B&B. The pottery and various articles found dated back to medieval times. It was thought that originally it could have been the site of a windmill but no sign of this was found when excavating. A medieval skeleton was dug up on the site in the summer of 2017.

Maids Moreton C of E Infant School, built in the 1960s to replace the Old School House in Main Street, is flourishing and villagers get involved in events held at the school. In May, a May Queen and May King are crowned and maypole dancing takes place.

We have various annual events in the village: a village barbecue in the church grounds, in October a Scarecrow Day where villagers display their scarecrows and people from all around come to visit and vote for the best, and then in December carol singing takes place around the village accompanied by a band. Maids Moreton WI, formed in 1957, is well known in the village and takes part in various local events.

Maids Moreton's contribution to the Millennium Celebrations was the staging of a pageant presenting scenes of village history, from the 1450 founding of the church up to the present day. We had a professional director, some professional help with music, the assistance of a professional

The Old Post Office in Maids Moreton

gunpowder handler from The Sealed Knot and participation of stunt riders from the local Devil's Horsemen. Villagers raised the funds, produced a script, acted, sang, danced, made costumes, props, and scenery. The Pageant, presented on the Church Green for three evenings in May 2000, attracted audiences from Buckingham, neighbouring villages and further afield; all tickets sold out for each performance. The event exemplified the strong community spirit of the village of Maids Moreton.

St Edmunds Church has recently been modernised and now has a kitchen and inside loo! This has enabled concerts and other events to be held in addition to the Sunday services. In the church porch, hoof prints supposedly from the time of a Civil War siege can be seen. An original north door, now kept in the tower, has musket holes also from that time.

🍁 MARLOW BOTTOM

Marlow Bottom can be found to the north of Marlow. Wycombe District in November 2007 recognised it as a civil parish in its own right, with a keen sense of its own identity and a strong feeling of community.

On arriving at the valley entrance, there is a rowing sculpture that was erected in May 2015 as a tribute to local hero Sir Steve Redgrave, famous for his five Olympic gold medals. He grew up in Marlow Bottom and was one of the first pupils of Burford County Combined primary school when it opened in 1972. Next you may be greeted with the distinct smell of hops from the Rebellion Brewery established in 1993. Its membership has increased to over 7,000 with well-attended monthly public open nights and a biennial Charity Weekend which raises thousands for the local scanner appeal.

Ahead there is a long winding road with housing estates rising from both sides. These developments were built in the mid-1960s and brought many changes with them. Mains gas and drainage were finally installed, making cesspits and septic tanks redundant. Marlow Bottom Road, previously a mainly unmade cart track, was widened, levelled out and tarmacked. By the 2011 census, the population had grown to 3,500. It is now recognised as a highly desirable residential area, with developers hovering to snap up the smallest plot of vacant land.

This is a far cry from when the valley was known as 'Tin Town'. Prior to the First World War, the 1911 census figures indicate there were four farms and 43 residents. But in 1921, an estate developer, Mr C J Brake, advertised 'Cheap Freehold Land' in the 'prettiest part of Buckinghamshire'. Plots with 20ft frontage and 200ft long were offered from £12 to £23, and they were purchased by Londoners and others from further afield. One man known as 'the Alpine Climber' lived in an improvised tent and was a familiar figure in tattered shorts, mountaineering sports coat and Tyrolean hat complete with feather. His friend 'Pixie' Poole described as a 'queer nattering woman' lived nearby in a caravan and kept a goat. Many of the other new settlers were do-it-yourself fans and with no disapproving planning officers to curb their eccentricities, a collection of ramshackle shacks of all shapes and sizes developed, made of timber and asbestos with corrugated iron roofs on which the sun glinted, hence the name 'Tin Town'. It was not felt to be a credit to its neighbour, Marlow.

At this time a rather mysterious sanatorium, probably constructed at the end of the 19th century and rumoured to have been used for the rehabilitation of drug addicts was sold as a private residence to Mrs Scott, described as 'a stately Edwardian lady'. In the late 1930s, she decided to build a tea room in the valley and called it the 'Witches Barn' with menu cards and china bearing the logo of a witch on a broomstick. She catered

Marlow Bottom Village Hall

Wilma Johnston.

for tourists enjoying a trip to the countryside, signposting the route from the Crown Hotel in Marlow.

Following the Second World War, the number of dwellings quickly increased to 750 by 1949, now built of brick in accordance with the 1947 Town and Country Planning Act. As the population grew, the central hub of the Valley was developed along the Marlow Bottom Road and this is where the Village Hall, the Barn Club and the Rose Industrial Estate are situated.

Sydney Folker led the plan to purchase and convert the vacant Witches Barn to the Village Hall in 1949. He was a flamboyant character who strode the valley 'in a black sombrero and long black cloak' and had starred in silent movies during the 1920s. As the first Village Hall Chairman, he produced plays, painted the scenery, prepared the programmes and acted on stage. However, there was no permit for alcohol consumption but this was overcome by a club licence being issued to use the old Nissen hut on the site, previously used by the land army girls as a canteen. The hut was renamed The Barn Club and it eventually moved to a brick-built premises in 1962.

The site of the small industrial estate was originally a working homestead producing grain, wheat, vegetables and rearing pigs until 1936 when 'Pop' Arnold brought it and successfully transformed the farm into a high-end furniture manufacturing business. Following his death in 1974, his sons sold to a Mr Rose, a flamboyant Canadian known for driving an open-top, pink Cadillac. Mr Rose developed the factory into individual units, sadly many of the farm barns were lost but the historic Great Tithe Barn survives to this day.

Fortunately the Valley has retained much of its green space and woodlands. The Residents Association ran several successful appeals in the 1980s for donations from residents raising over £35,000, enabling the Woodland Trust to purchase three areas of woodland, which are now protected. An additional bonus is the playing field adjacent to the school, bought by the Parish Council in 1970. The site's upkeep was supported by funds raised by the annual Rose Carnival. However, in 2012 the carnival was replaced with an open-air music event. The first 'Rock Bottom' in 2013 was a success and is now an annual event for all the family.

Another successful charity event, started in 1999, is the Shepherd family's Christmas lights – they turn their house into an amazing magical sound and light show throughout December. It takes 82 hours to put up 33,000 Christmas lights and 20 hours of programming for each song.

🍁 MARLOW-ON-THAMES

The picturesque town of Marlow is nestled at the foothills of the Chilterns and situated on a broad reach of the River Thames between Henley and Windsor. Its population is approximately 26,000 people and there is easy access to the M40, M4 and M25 motorways and a branch rail connection via Maidenhead to central London.

The vibrant, affluent town has a wide range of restaurants from Michelin-starred to fast food chains, plus coffee shops, a myriad of pubs, and boutique clothes shops which entice droves of tourists into the town. The historic streets have been home to Jerome K. Jerome, T.S. Eliot and Mary and Percy Shelley.

The town's landmark is the iconic suspension bridge which spans the River Thames between the counties of Buckinghamshire and Berkshire. The bridge was designed by the engineer, William Tierney Clark, who built the bridge as a prototype for his Chain Bridge in Budapest, Hungary. As a result of this connection, the town is twinned with Budapest and also, Marly le Roi, near Paris, where close associations with both towns have been forged for many years.

This beautiful stretch of the river attracts boat owners, passenger steamers, rowers and walkers along the Thames Path during the summer months. Marlow Rowing Club has produced some fine Olympic oarsmen and women, including Sir Steve Redgrave and Dame Katherine Grainger, who live in or near the town. Marlow Regatta in June is a popular sporting and social occasion which features traditional rowing competitions but also raft and dragon boat racing, together with a canoe regatta. Pimm's, blazers, boaters and pretty summer dresses are the order of the day at celebratory picnics along the Thames.

The place to meet is Higginson Park where nearly every weekend during the summer there is a fete, carnival, music extravaganza, fun fair, playground or just a stroll along the riverside promenade with an ice cream! Marlow Lock also attracts visitors with stunning views of the river and weir, the bridge, the church and the Compleat Angler Hotel all in one view.

Marlow encourages participation in sport and boasts rugby, football, cricket, tennis, rowing, golf and hockey clubs. There are two fitness clubs, a water sports centre and just across the river the National Sports Centre at Bisham Abbey.

Marlow has a very cosmopolitan population and attracts young families

Marlow Rebellion Brewery

with good schools, including the popular Sir William Borlase's Grammar School. But there is something on offer for all ages, including a variety of activities with the U3A, Marlow National Trust Association, luncheon clubs, bridge clubs, Women's Institute, a variety of churches of all denominations and Marlow Age UK.

Going back in the past, Marlow was the home of the Whitbread Brewery which has now been converted into town houses and flats but retains the cobblestone streets where horses pulld drays loaded with barrels of beer. The Remnantz mansion in West Street was the first Royal Military Academy for junior officers before it was moved to Sandhurst, and the Compleat Angler Hotel on the banks of the Thames has hosted a plethora of distinguished guests throughout its 350-year history. Every July, the Queen's Swan Uppers, in all their colourful regalia, descend on the hotel to ring the cygnets who lawfully belong to the Crown. Bobbin lacemaking, thimbles and 'Poppit' beads are all associated with Marlow.

A very pleasant town to live in, work and socialise.

🍁 MARSWORTH

The Grand Union Canal runs through Marsworth with an arm of the canal going off to Aylesbury. The village is surrounded by farming country and was part of Lord Rosebery's estate. In the 1800s, it had its own hospital but this was demolished in 1894 and the land is now known as Hospital Farm.

An elderly resident remembers trains on a branch line to Aylesbury stopping at Marston Gate. They would stop just outside the village to pick up milk brought in from the surrounding farms for the Nestlé milk factory at Aylesbury.

The canal was very busy at the beginning of the 20th century with boats carrying coal, sand and wheat. In 1916, the canal froze over for six weeks and there was no movement of traffic at all with boats stuck in the ice.

In the Second World War, Marsworth was used as an airfield. The RAF flew Wellington bombers out of here, and they were followed by 4,000 American airmen who flew Fortresses and Liberators. A leaflet squadron

The Grand Union Canal near Marsworth

was based here with a hospital, dining hall seating over 1000, and a theatre. The stage from the theatre was then put into the village hall once the war was over.

There was also an underground command post on the airfield. It was reported to be as big as a good-sized bungalow and to be bombproof. It was kept well stocked with food and water at all times. Churchill was a regular visitor particularly towards the end of the war. He used to land there on his way to Chequers. General Patten also visited Marsworth and decorated some of the American airmen during a service held at the camp.

Although Marsworth has grown since those wartime years, it is still a very happy and friendly place to live.

☙ MEDMENHAM

The picturesque village of Medmenham nestles in the lee of Wooded Hill to the north and is principally a street of brick and flint cottages which straggles from the former ferry on the River Thames to its junction with the main Henley-Marlow road half a mile away. The cottages and houses were built for the servants of the nearby large houses and estates such as Medmenham Abbey, Danesfield, Wittington, Kingswood and Harleyford Manor.

At the junction of Ferry Lane and the main road is the ancient parish church of St Peter & St Paul, and opposite is The Dog & Badger, a recently refurbished 14th-century inn.

Danesfield House, an imposing residence built in 1900 on a cliff overlooking the Thames, was occupied by the Royal Air Force until 1977 and is now a luxury hotel and spa.

The original Danesfield House was built in 1750 on a site previously occupied by Medlicotts, during the Middle Ages. A tradition had grown up locally associating the prehistoric earthworks in the grounds with the Danes who were known to have penetrated the Thames Valley as far as Reading, some 15 miles further upstream. In 1896, the Medmenham Abbey Estate was acquired by Mr Robert Hudson, reputed to have made his fortune with Hudson's Soap.

At the foot of Ferry Lane stands Medmenham Abbey, founded as St Mary's Abbey by the Cistercian Order in the 13th century. It later became derelict. However, in the 18th century Sir Francis Dashwood restored the Abbey and it is said to have been used by his 'Hell Fire Club'

Medmenham Abbey

for orgiastic rites. It is now a fine residence overlooking a pretty reach of the river.

🍁 MONKS RISBOROUGH

The White Cross cut into the chalk of the Chiltern Escarpment is visible for many miles from the Vale of Aylesbury. Tucked in the valley below lies the unique village of Monks Risborough, unique because the parish has the distinction of being the oldest in England.

Documents, now in the British Museum, state that the land at East Risborough ('the brush-covered hills') was conveyed by Aethelfrith to his daughter Etheigyth in AD 903. The original documents were destroyed by fire. The boundary is recorded and several landmarks – both the black hedge and the Icknield Way – mentioned in the Charter can still be identified. The parish of Monks Risborough also contains the hamlets of Owlswick, Meadle, with its strong Quaker connections, Askett and Whiteleaf. The tradition of Beating the Bounds took place in 1975 and in 2003, the 1100th anniversary of the Charter, by walking or horse riding.

By the time of the Domesday Survey in 1086, the land was in the possession of the monks of Christ Church, Canterbury (hence the name Monks) and there it remained until the Dissolution of the Monasteries by Henry VIII. It is now under the See of Oxford.

A recent dig turned up remains that point to the foundations of the parish church, St Dunstan's, dating back to the 11th century. The tower and roof are Norman, and areas of the interior show signs of damage by Cromwell's troops during the Civil War. Inside is an 11th-century Aylesbury Font, a slate sculpture of St Dunstan, a stained-glass window dedicated to Samuel Wilberforce who came to the village when Bishop of Oxford, and early paintings of prophets on a wooden screen. In addition to Sunday and weekday services, the church is used for flower shows, showing exhibits during the annual Bucks Art Weeks, various concerts and film shows and is used by the local C of E primary school.

The church stands within the village's conservation area. This includes the Victorian school and former schoolmaster's house, the old rectory built in 1670, a 16th-century dovecote, an 18th-century farmhouse and various cottages, the latter much photographed and painted. The dovecote, built of coursed chalk rubble, is unusual because of the way in which the 216 cotes are positioned.

The land for the school was given by St Dunstan's in 1840. It was built for £300 and is a thriving school to this day. The school logs go back to at least 1865, recording outbreaks of measles, an outbreak of diphtheria which shut the school for a month, haymaking, blackberry picking for the WI and the death of old boys in the First World War.

The boundary between Monks Risborough and Princes Risborough is now blurred, with extensive building of houses and bungalows taking place in the 1950s including a shopping parade.

In earlier times, Monks Risborough was a busy working village with Hundred Acres Farm (now Chestnut Farmhouse), the Nags Head pub, a busy bakery, general shop, saddler's, blacksmith and a butcher's with a slaughterhouse behind. The cottages were occupied by farm labourers, small tradespeople and women involved in the making of Buckinghamshire lace.

The bakery was situated in what is now Bakehouse Cottage in Burton Lane, the family living on the premises. About 6,500 loaves of bread were produced each week with deliveries to local villages and also to Chequers. On Christmas Day, the bakery would roast the villagers' turkeys at a charge of two shillings per bird. Opposite Bakehouse Cottage was a shop, owned by the family, selling almost everything.

The house now called Saddlers facing the church, in Burton Lane, made harnesses and sold anything to do with horses. Ropes of all sizes were made there too, there being a 'ropewalk' in the grounds.

Burton Lane runs into what is now a lay-by off the Aylesbury Road and at one corner stands the old Blacksmith's Forge and Shop. Opposite the Forge stood The Nags Head, now a private house, originally owned by Benskins Brewery.

At the opposite end of the lay-by to Chestnut Farm stood the butcher's shop with a large arch under which animals were taken to a slaughterhouse. A humane killer was used for horses, with a tan pit used for tanning their hides. This area is now a car park for a dental practice.

Monks Risborough has two halls, one owned by the church, the other by Monks Risborough WI and both are used for various classes, groups and for social events. For the Millennium, a large wall hanging was made by the WI members showing the most interesting features of the village and it is registered with the National Needlework Record's Stitch 2000 project. Most of the members contributed with a very varied use of techniques including knitting, felt, stump and ribbon work, fabric painting and embroidery. This was made with a grant under the Millennium Festival Awards for All Programme.

The village unites over the well-attended annual Horticultural Show staged by the local Society, the annual Kop Hill Climb which passes through the village, and the well-used local Green Bus.

🍁 NAPHILL & WALTERS ASH

These two adjacent villages are in the Chilterns AONB and whichever way you approach them you have to come up a hill. One way is up from Hughenden Valley, the other is up from the village of Bradenham. Both villages were home to the D'Israeli family – Bradenham Manor was home to Isaac D'Israeli and it was there that his son Benjamin grew up. He married Mary Ann and after his father died they moved to Hughenden Manor. He became Prime Minister and a friend to Queen Victoria, who visited him several times at Hughenden. Both Bradenham and Hughenden have very old churches and Benjamin D'Israeli's grave is in Hughenden churchyard. Both estates are now owned by the National Trust.

Naphill and part of Walters Ash are in the parish of Hughenden and a large part of Naphill land was once owned by the Hughenden Estate. After D'Israeli died in 1881 and his brother Ralph in 1898, Benjamin's nephew Major Coningsby D'Israeli moved to Hughenden and became Squire of the village. At this time, Naphill did not have a village hall. The villagers did lots of fundraising and eventually enough had been raised for one to be built. Coningsby D'Israeli gave the ground for the playing fields and our village hall, which was opened in 1928 by Major and Mrs D'Israeli. Over the years, the hall has been extended with central heating added. It is well used every day by different organisations, including Naphill Evening WI. It really is the focal point of the village, especially as part of it is now the Bon Ami cafe, a very popular meeting place. Outside on the corner is our War Memorial, which is built in the form of a cairn made from local stone. The names of Naphill men who lost their lives are remembered every year in a service on Remembrance Sunday.

Originally twice the size, Naphill has a very old common of some 155 acres. It was open grassland with a few trees enclosed by banks and ditches to contain the animals that were grazed there. This ended in the 1920s and the common has now evolved to mixed woodland. In 1951, it was declared an SSSI Grade 1 (Site of Special Scientific Interest). Naphill has the largest wooded common in Buckinghamshire and we are fortunate to have a local society dedicated to its conservation.

There are several rows of old flint cottages in Naphill. Originally the villages were all farms, with 14 known from the 17th to early 19th century. In the late 1800s/early 1900s, the village became known for its stone cutters. They found some very large stones which took 20 men to haul out. In the early 1900s, our local sandstone was taken by horse-drawn wagons to Windsor for renovations to the castle. There were also the brickmakers yards, which gave work to the men of the village. This once flourishing industry ceased in the 1950s, but the sandstone side of the business was run for many years by J. Smith and Sons, the road contractors, who employed many local men.

RAF High Wycombe is based in Walters Ash and it houses Headquarters Air Command. We have officers from all around the world there – a very important place. It was in the late 1930s with war increasingly likely that plans were drawn up for RAF Bomber Command Headquarters at Walters Ash. The site was selected for its remoteness and the buildings disguised, so that from the air it was not possible to guess its role or significance. Sir Arthur 'Bomber' Harris was appointed the Commanding Officer in 1942.

One of Naphill's famous residents was Dilly Knox of Bletchley Park fame, who was awarded the CMG by the King for his work breaking the German coding in WW2 and also in WW1. In front of the village hall, we have a tree given by Dilly which was planted in 1937 to mark the coronation of King George VI. Every Christmas, the tree was decorated by local resident Mr Don Ing who owned an electrical shop in High Wycombe. In 1964, Don and his wife were tragically killed in a plane crash so we still decorate the tree every Christmas to this day in their memory. Another well known local was the model Jean Shrimpton (known as 'The Shrimp'), who was the first person to wear the miniskirt. On a darker note, in 1992 a notorious murder was committed. A millionaire resident disappeared and his body was never found. His former business partner was convicted but has always maintained his innocence.

The annual village fete has been outgrown and replaced by the 'Napfest' weekend. On Friday night, there is music with live bands, followed on Saturday by our fete. The WI do teas and cakes and the RAF now play a major role and combine it with their Family Day. On Sunday, there is a classic car show and although this raises funds for the Air Ambulance, proceeds from the Friday and Saturday events are for village hall funds.

Most of the events taking place are reported in our monthly magazine the 'Naphill and Walters Ash Gazette'. It is a very popular place for local businesses to advertise and keeps everyone up to date with what is going on. There is no need for anyone in the village to be lonely as there are so many organisations to join. There are two pubs, various shops and we are on a good bus route. It is a very happy and lively place to live.

🍁 NEWPORT PAGNELL

The vibrant historic market town of Newport Pagnell is situated in north-east Buckinghamshire, between the Ouse and Lovat rivers. It is a thriving town, with a fabulous history, a great community spirit and its own

Mayor. We have a range of shops, from traditional to the modern, and a Farmers' Market which takes place every month. We certainly have a fair share of restaurants and pubs, and there are plenty of places to go to meet up with family and friends. Going back around 100 years, there were over 30 licensed premises in the town, many of which were originally coaching inns.

Events take place throughout the year, organised and supported by committed teams of volunteers. As well as smaller fairs, our event highlights are the Summer Festival, Strawberry Fair, July Carnival, Soap Box Derby, Remembrance Day Parade, and Christmas Fayre. The Carnival features floats decorated according to the theme for the year, as well as vintage cars and bikes. Our Christmas lights, paid for by donations from residents, are turned on at the Christmas Fayre. Every event is always well-attended, bringing in visitors from the surrounding area and beyond.

Newport Pagnell has existed since before the Iron Age. It is mentioned in the 1086 Domesday Book. Originally called Neuport, meaning 'New Market Town', it took on the name of feudal lord Fulk Paynell in the 12th century. Paynell was given the land by William the Conqueror, and was closely associated with the town, the family having founded a Priory here.

During the Civil War, the town became a garrison for Parliamentary forces. The essential road links made it an asset to hold. If you wander over to Bury Common, you can still see some remains of the earthwork defences that were put in place. John Bunyan served here as a garrison officer, and it is thought Oliver Cromwell's son died of smallpox in the town.

Later in its history, Newport Pagnell became the centre of the lace industry. It was thought that more bone lace was made here than in any other town in Britain.

Newport Pagnell is probably better known as a buzzing transport centre. We were, after all, the location of the first motorway service station. The town has always been a direct route for Leicester, London, Oxford and Cambridge. The increase in traffic brought prosperity to the town, as coaching inns began to spring up to cater for those passing through. The early 19th century saw the building of two major bridges to cope with the increasing traffic. Today, Tickford Bridge is one of the few remaining working iron bridges in the country.

Newport Pagnell is proud to be the home of car company Aston Martin, which was established here in the 1950s. Our town has an even older history in luxury vehicles, which dates back to 1830. Joseph Salmons became famous for coach building. Salmons & Sons later progressed to coach-built cars, and then to building car bodies and developing innovative car hood designs. The company changed its name over the years. In the 1950s, it was eventually bought by David Brown and became part of Aston Martin Lagonda Ltd. Aston Martin has been visited by the Queen and Prince Charles. Several James Bond cars have been built here, including the Goldfinger DB5 and the Vanquish from *Die Another Day.*

One perhaps lesser known fact is that Newport Pagnell is the home to the only remaining vellum paper manufacturer in the UK. Established in 1870, William Cowley Parchment is a family business, passing trade skills down through the generations. Vellum produced here is still used for Royal and Government documents.

> *'Our town has been proud to have the WI as a valuable part of our community for over 60 years. While society has evolved, they remain as relevant today as they have ever been, and we hope they continue for many years to come.'*
>
> Cllr Paul Day, Mayor of Newport Pagnell

 OAKLEY

Like many English settlements, Oakley – situated between Thame and Bicester – has its first written mention in the Domesday Book of 1086. The name Oakley derives from the Old English words 'ac' and 'leah', meaning 'oak clearing'. The name has been spelled in various ways, from Achelei in 1086, through to Akeley in the 12th century and Whokeley in the 16th century.

Throughout the centuries, Oakley has gradually evolved from an entirely agricultural village to one in which many villagers now work in places like Thame, Bicester and Oxford.

Nevertheless, the story of developing Oakley can still be observed – Oakley House, a hunting lodge rebuilt after fire damage in 1660, Paddock Cottage with the external rounded back of a bread oven still visible, the Old Forge dated 1892 and of course St Mary's Church, part of which dates back to the 12th century.

Oakley airfield was opened in 1942 as the satellite station to RAF

Westcott. By Autumn 1943, when the RAF Operational Training Unit and Vickers Wellington aircraft were based at RAF Westcott, Oakley's primary role was conversion training for bomber crews – a role which continued until the end of the war.

During Operation Exodus, which began on 2 May 1945, the first 300 repatriated prisoners of war arrived and were met by the village children who had saved up their sweet rations as a homecoming present. By the end of the month, Oakley had seen the repatriation of more than 15,000 personnel.

One of the two remaining hangars on the airfield featured in the opening sequence of Bond film *Octopussy* and the airfield has also been used as a location for *Midsomer Murders*.

The inhabitants of Oakley are very fortunate to benefit from several charities, the largest of which is Oakley Relief In Need Charity. This can trace its origins back to the closing years of the reign of James I when Brill, Boarstall and Oakley were deep in the heart of Bernwood Forest. James I was short of money and so he set about a policy of disafforestation in 1624, to swell the royal coffers. Lords of the Manor, freeholders and the inhabitants of the villages were all given allowances of land in lieu of their rights of common. The land was to be held for the benefit of the poorer inhabitants of the three parishes.

Today, Oakley Relief In Need Charity owns approximately 94 acres of land in the parish of Oakley which are let to local farmers for agricultural use and to the village Allotment Society. The Trustees of the Charity meet twice a year (or more often if necessary) to consider any requests for help. In addition, the Charity finances the village hospital transport scheme, aid-call emergency pendants for those living alone, Christmas parcels to pensioners, plus grants to village university students and apprentices.

Edward Brooks, one of only two Buckinghamshire Victoria Cross holders, was born in Oakley in 1883, the sixth of thirteen children. He was awarded the V.C. for his courageous actions in April 1917 when, as a Company Sergeant Major, he captured an enemy machine gun at Fayet, near Saint-Quentin. On the 100th anniversary of his brave actions, a ceremony was held in the village and a commemorative stone placed at the side of the Oakley war memorial in the presence of the Lord Lieutenant of Buckinghamshire, the Mayor of Fayet and other dignitaries.

Doreen West, who for many years lived in the village, became a bestselling author in her seventies when she wrote *Louie: A Country Lady* (published in 1997) about her mother's life through two World Wars in

Oakley and later Oxford. Doreen is also remembered for providing a horse and cart each Christmas to enable Father Christmas and the children of Oakley School to deliver gift parcels – for which they had saved during the year – to the elderly in the village.

In 1963, Oakley hit the headlines when Leatherslade Farm, just outside the village, was used as a hideout by the criminal gang involved in the Great Train Robbery. The only clue to their whereabouts was the fact that the farm drive, which opens onto the Oakley-Thame road, was shut and padlocked for the first time. A local resident noticed and reported this, and two days later a local policeman checked it out and found the robbers' hideaway. In 2003, Oakley again featured in the news when an exhibition marking the 40th anniversary of the Great Train Robbery was held. One of the guest speakers was Bruce Reynolds, the mastermind behind the crime.

Over the years, Oakley has been home to several well-known people, including the artist James Henry Govier, Colin and Jonny Greenwood of Radiohead fame, Max Moseley president of the Fédération Internationale de l'Automobile, and TV star David Icke.

🍁 OLNEY

Olney is a small rural market town with a rich history. Sitting on the banks of the River Great Ouse in the far north of Buckinghamshire, the town is just two miles from the borders with both Bedfordshire and Northamptonshire. Olney was once a thriving Roman settlement. In a Saxon charter from AD 979, it is named Ollanege ('ege', meaning 'island', was pronounced 'ey' in Old English). We were mentioned in the Domesday Book, and Olney Bridge was the scene of a Parliamentarian victory in 1643, during the English Civil War.

These days, we are perhaps most famous for the Olney Pancake Race, held on Shrove Tuesday each year since 1445. The legend tells of a housewife being late for the shriving service at our parish church and running from her home with a pancake in her frying pan still in her hand. To mark the story, the women of Olney make the 415-yard dash to the church each year, as part of a day filled with other racing and eating fun in our Market Place. The schoolchildren of Olney have their own races and participation requires them to be dressed in full housewife costume with a pancake in their frying pan. Talk of technique and tactics is rife as all entrants must flip their pancakes as they run and cross the finish line. If your frying pan is empty at the finish, sadly you are disqualified. Friendly rivalry in the village is common and some ladies train for weeks in advance! Indeed, the event is now so popular that visitors to Olney can order pancakes at any time of year in our teashops, cafés or at The Pancake Parlour.

Olney's most famous former residents are William Cowper and John Newton, composers of the beloved hymn *Amazing Grace*. An award-winning museum now fills the former home of celebrated 18th-century poet William Cowper. John Newton, a prominent slave trade abolitionist, became the curate of the local church here. The vicarage garden backed onto Cowper's garden and the two went on to forge a great friendship. Together they penned a divinely inspired body of work entitled the *Olney Hymns*, which included *Amazing Grace*.

John Newton's tomb can be visited today in Olney churchyard. It is wonderful when travelling far from home to hear *Amazing Grace* being played or sung – it immediately transports one back to Olney, this little haven by the water where the community spirit is palpable and all are welcomed.

🍁 PADBURY

Padbury – from Padda's burgh meaning 'Padda's township – sits on a tributary of the River Ouse, known as the River Lovat but named on maps as Padbury Brook. We have the site of an Iron Age fort, which was visible until the land was cultivated during the Second World War, a water mill and the site of a windmill, which was planted as The Millennium Wood in 1999. The main London to Banbury road skirted the village using what is now just a country lane. You can still see the 'ridge and furrow' strips made by farmers ploughing the land in the Middle Ages. At one time the whole village was owned by All Souls College, Oxford. Now only a few properties are still in their possession.

We are fortunate to still have a thriving village school, a 13th-century church, an active sports field, currently only one pub and a butcher's. We lost our post office in the major cutbacks a few years ago. However, most activity centres round the Village Hall which uses the early Victorian school building in the centre of the village.

One of our claims to fame is having one of the oldest 'insurance' societies in the country still in existence. The Padbury Sick Benefit Society (PSBS) dates back to 1856 but was a successor to the earlier Padbury and Hillesden Friendly Society. The original aims of the society were to support the many farm labourers and others during illness or after accidents. The Society still thrives and has an annual celebration at the end of May which involves a dance in the Village Hall, a church service, a march with a brass band and a fabulous meal for members in the Village Hall. But it isn't all celebration, the members still do support one another and other village causes.

Like many villages we have had our characters and tales abound of horses taking their drunken master home, or ditching them in the river. Many villagers learned to swim in a pool at the bend of the river. One centenarian was buried with the bell rope that he had used in the church tower for many years. Fortunately much of this history was preserved when *The Padbury Book* was published for the Millennium.

Although still surrounded by farmland, the village now has only two working farms plus a smallholding of rare breed sheep and cattle. We have artists, musicians, a film director and a florist, and of course some people work from home on a regular basis. We are fortunate too, to have one-man businesses, an electrician, a plumber a builder and some gardeners. What more could you want? The housing ranges from late 16th-century properties to 21st-century homes, with

Padbury

another small development imminent. Many older properties have thatched roofs.

Although we are a diverse community of ancient and new families, all are welcomed, especially if they want to contribute to village life. There are over twenty groups that can be accessed, ranging from the church, school and allotments to book clubs, the WI and those who love to play whist and bingo. There are various annual Fetes and Fairs and a Produce Show every September, where villagers old and new, young and old vie to have the biggest and best. Padbury really is a wonderful place to live.

Penn & Tylers Green

Penn and Tylers Green are two adjoining villages, united by a close-knit community spirit and facilities that serve residents of both villages. Penn pre-dates Tylers Green but is a very small hamlet with a few houses. Tylers Green, originally Tylers End, is where many of the famous Penn Tiles were made in the 14th century. These were highly prized tiles and lie in, amongst other places, St George's Chapel at Windsor. A pavement formed of broken tiles may be seen in Holy Trinity Church, Penn opposite the Crown pub (not to be confused with the Victorian church in Tylers Green). Indeed, this Grade I listed building is not to be missed. Tile fragments are still found in the fields today and recent housing developments unearthed at least two more kilns, one dating back to the 14th century, bringing the total known number to at least fifteen. Sadly after a short, interesting, viewing interval they were built over.

The centre of outdoor activities is the Front Common, which is the area around the pond. A Fun Run and quarter marathon, the Penn Seven, start and finish here each year. The Fun Run was started by a local couple in 1984 hoping to raise money in memory of their five-year-old daughter, who tragically died from leukaemia. Since then, the run has raised many thousands of pounds for local charities. The First School uses the Common for maypole dancing and each year villagers join in 'Carols on the Common' a few nights before Christmas. The Millennium celebrations took place here on a misty night with the sky resembling something out of a Turner painting with the mixture of mist and fireworks.

By contrast, the Back Common provides a semi-wild area for walking, playing games and other outdoor activities. It includes 30 memorial trees planted in memory of the fallen and each year, a Remembrance Service is held amidst them on 11 November.

In living memory, both Penn and Tylers Green have had a variety of shops and businesses; villagers did not need to go further afield for their everyday items. These included a very popular general outfitter, a shoe shop, which later became the Old Horology Shop, and at one time four butchers. Up until 2018, there was a world-renowned second-hand bookshop in the row of old cottages near the Red Lion pub. This small cottage held 60,000 books stacked in double rows and once in, it was a job to find your way out, such was the rabbit warren of bookshelves! Nowadays, two small supermarkets, a butcher, a pharmacy, four pubs, a delicatessen/coffee shop, a hairdresser's, a dry cleaner's and a stringed instruments shop serve the villages.

The villages frequently feature in TV programmes. At the time of writing, an episode from *Endeavour* is being filmed here so a small part of the village has been temporarily moved to Oxfordshire! Before that, we had the pleasure of being in Cambridgeshire somewhere near Grantchester. There is a vintage car garage just beyond the pond on the way to Beaconsfield which frequently attracts admirers and film crews wishing to borrow vintage cars.

Locals refer to Penn and Tylers Green as 'the village'. However there are some strange anomalies. Penn lies in a different district council and parliamentary constituency to Tylers Green. Older residents remember the days when, due to two pubs on opposite sides of the road being in different licensing authorities, every Friday and Saturday night customers of the Red Lion would leave at closing time, cross the road and enter the Horse and Groom to enjoy an extra half an hour of alcohol. There was even a pub, now a private house, which had a boundary line marked on the bar as it sat astride the civic boundary!

But the introduction of internet address finders has merged the two villages into one postal area, Penn, as the creators of these drop-down lists decided to use the word Penn instead of Tylers Green for all addresses in Tylers Green.

The villages are surrounded by beautiful countryside and extensive woods, providing many walking opportunities. The oldest beech trees are roughly 200 years old and were planted when furniture making was a major industry in High Wycombe. In those days, bodgers (chair turners) set up workshops in the woods. There is also ample evidence of villagers digging for flint for the local houses and clay for the famous tiles. Common Wood, believed to have been the site of a Roman settlement, adjoins Penn Wood to form one of the largest 'ancient woodlands' in the Chilterns Area of Outstanding Natural Beauty, containing several rare plants and interesting fauna.

The village has been fortunate in having a local historian, Miles Green, who has researched and written several books and pamphlets on the many noteworthy buildings and interesting, occasionally notorious, people who have been associated with Penn and Tylers Green.

🍁 Pitstone

Pitstone can trace its origins right back to the Iron Age. Excavations on Pitstone Hill and surrounding areas have revealed traces of a settlement as early as 250BC. Pitstone Museum, which is open to the public on certain days throughout the year, houses many fascinating relics from the village's past. College Lake, on the site of the old Quarry 3 of the Cement Works, has exhibits of fossilised animals, including mammoths, which also testify to our past.

In the 11th century, Pitstone was known as Pincenestorne but over the years the name was shortened to the one we use today. The beautiful church of St. Mary the Virgin was founded in AD 1180 and, although not in regular use, special events still take place there.

One of the most iconic landmarks in Pitstone is the Windmill which dates from 1627 and which, after falling into disrepair, is now owned and run by the National Trust.

We cannot mention Pitstone without reference to the Cement Works which thrived here from 1936 until 1991. It was set up by a Danish firm and created much-needed employment in the community.

It was named Tunnel Cement but changed ownership several times and was renamed Castle Cement in 1986. The works closed in 1991 but the tall chimneys were not demolished until 1999 prior to the site being cleared for the new estate. The new development which consisted of industrial and residential areas was called Castlemead as a tribute to its former occupants.

Modern Pitstone is a thriving village with a village hall complex which offers a variety of social and recreational activities for the community. The Green has a well-used area for children as well as cricket and football pitches which feature regular matches during the appropriate seasons.

The local shop is a focal point for the village. Every year in early November, one of our villagers, Joe Marling, parks his Second World War Jeep outside the shop and collects money for the Royal British Legion.

He is a very popular figure who raises hundreds of pounds each year, running into thousands over the time he has been there. He is always ready with a quip to entice you to buy a poppy.

The residents of Church Road put on a wonderful display of Christmas Lights for all and raise money for charity.

We have an Allotment Society which runs our very popular allotments.

We share many facilities with our neighbours Ivinghoe – our wonderful WI is a good example of this.

An Over 60s Club and a Tuesday afternoon club meet in the Yardley Avenue Centre for the benefit of the elderly in both villages. The Guides and Scouts are also a shared enterprise.

Pitstone is a friendly, caring community which is welcoming to new residents and visitors alike.

🍁 PRESTWOOD

Prestwood, meaning 'priest's wood', is a village in the Chiltern Hills, about two miles west of Great Missenden. There is evidence of settlement here from the Middle Ages, when the village was mainly covered in oak, beech and ash trees.

But by 1849, much of the woodland was cleared to create common land. Our population now stands at roughly 9,000 and there is small-scale development that still goes on.

Prestwood WI was founded in 1924. They decided they needed a hall in which to meet so a committee was formed to raise funds and it is recorded that every door in the village was knocked on. The foundation stone was laid on 7 June 1928 by the Countess of Macclesfield and on 18 October 1928, the WI handed the Hall over to the village as a Village Hall with Trustees, two of whom are WI members. The Hall is in constant use by various local organisations, during the day this is mainly exercise classes, weekly lunches and of course, the two WIs. At weekends there are fund-raising events such as jumble sales, craft fairs, dances and quizzes etc. The Evening WI Craft Group have produced a wall hanging for the Village Hall, depicting scenes around the village.

Over the last few years, the village has lost its bank and petrol station, but still has a post office offering a full range of services, as well as newspapers, groceries etc. Sainsbury's and the Co-Op have local stores, and there is a butcher's shop, fish and chips shop, three pubs, two hairdresser's, florists, two doctors' and two dentists' surgeries, as well as various practitioners of alternative therapies, such as physio and reflexology.

There are several family businesses which have been trading here for many years. Hildreths, which comprises a garden centre, hardware shop, kitchen and homeware department, started over 400 years ago as a blacksmith's – and the present proprietor is Richard Hildreth XIII. Wren Davis Farm, which began milk deliveries in 1923 from Collings Hanger Farm on the Wycombe Road, still delivers milk in glass bottles (as well as other dairy and grocery products) around the area. On their site is also Malt the Brewery, started a few years ago, which regularly wins prizes for home-brewed beers. The Brill family moved to Peterley Manor Farm over 30 years ago and people from far and wide descend on the farm every summer to 'pick their own' strawberries, raspberries and other fruit. The farm shop sells a wide range of goods and hundreds of Christmas trees are sold every December. The Yurt at Peterley is another popular eating place, with tables outside in good weather and various workshops, special event meals, and parties catered for, organised by Katie and Pippa Brill.

In 2016, Holy Trinity Church, built in 1849, was completely reordered, thanks to a very generous bequest from a former parishioner, and much local fundraising. This beautiful church now has underfloor heating, light wooden chairs and bench pews, a movable altar plus a new organ, lighting and sound systems. The church now provides a friendly open space which is used not only for services but for social events, concerts, Toddlers Group, Rock Band and many parties. Other denominations in the village are the Methodist Church in the High Street and The Kings Church meeting in the Village Hall.

The local Colts Football Club for boys and girls celebrated its 50th birthday in 2018 and Sprinters Sports Centre provides facilities for tennis and cricket and a full gym. The Abbey Gymnastics Club hopes to build their own premises in the near future, catering for children, teenagers and eventually adults. Several walking groups meet weekly or monthly to explore the beautiful countryside around the area. Guides, Scouts and their junior sections meet in their respective huts on Prestwood Common.

There is also a community centre, now run by the Parish Council and hired by various local organisations.

The Infant School in Moat Lane was built in 1908 and has had several modern additions over the years. The Junior School, opened in 1969 when a large housing estate was developed, has recently celebrated its 50th birthday. From here, the children progress to various senior schools in the area. In 2018, the administration of the two schools was merged under one head teacher.

The Prestwood Village Association and Prestwood Events Group both keep locals in touch with what is going on and organise social and information events from time to time. *The Source HP16* is a local community-produced tabloid publication, giving updates on local activities, events, businesses etc. and is delivered free to every house in the HP16 postal area by a team of local volunteers every two months.

Prestwood also has a charity shop, which we think is unique because all the money raised by the volunteer team who run it is passed to local charities and organisations, such as schools, youth groups, churches and clubs for senior citizens. We are proud to say that since opening in 2010, well over £400,000 has been distributed to worthy causes on our doorstep.

🍁 PRINCES RISBOROUGH

Princes Risborough is a market town lying close to The Chiltern Hills and overlooked by The Whiteleaf Cross. The Domesday Book tells us that the Royal Manor of Princes Risborough belonged to Edward the Black Prince – and this gives the town part of its name. 'Risborough' is said to derive from the Old English 'hrisen + beorg', meaning 'brush-covered hills'.

The Royal Manor is gone now and locals recall the site was farmland – and home to a horse called Morgan – until The Mount car park was built.

The Whiteleaf Cross, dug out of the chalk escarpment overlooking the town, has unknown origins but was probably created in the 17th century. Several artists have painted it, the most well-known being Paul Nash.

The newly restored Market House in the centre of the town has origins

Princes Risborough

in the 18th century, and a weekly market is still held here.

Until a few years ago, Risborough, as locals call it, was a village with local trades recorded as lacemaking, paper making, boot making, brewing, tiling and baking. In 1830, the population was recorded as around 2,000 people yet that had climbed to around 8,000 by the census of 2011.

Residents during the 1950s recall a cobbled high street and a horse-drawn coal delivery in Church Street. Children would wait to see the coal horse returning to his stable as a treat.

Now, the high street has barbers, a dry cleaner, a pet shop, two opticians, 7 charity shops, four estate agents, a family-run shoe shop and three beauty salons. There is still a butcher but the fishmonger is long gone. In essence, the shops nowadays supply services which for the main can't be provided online.

Amy Johnson, the noted pilot, once lived here for a short while in Church Lane. Writer Winifred Holtby, the author of *South Riding*, stayed locally, and the artist and wood engraver Claire Leighton lived on the road to Whiteleaf, a small hamlet just outside Princes Risborough, in the 1930s. Other famous residents have included singer Sarah Harding, musician Jay Kay and the broadcaster Nicholas Parsons.

The Chilterns to the north of Risborough offer a great place to walk and enjoy the countryside with the Icknield Way popular with locals and visitors alike. Every year a town festival is held in the summer with all local groups and societies putting on a very good show. In September, the Kop Hill Climb is held with vintage cars climbing Kop Hill. This is now attracting cars from all over the country with money raised going to local charities.

Gone are the days when cows walked along the high street, but in the 21st century Princes Risborough is still proving to be an attractive and friendly place to live, with many residents deciding to spend their whole lives here.

❧ QUAINTON

Situated on the southern flank of hills, the centre of the village is the green with its stone cross which is thought to be a preaching cross erected in Saxon times before the church was built. A prominent feature is the windmill designed and built by a local man, James Anstiss, in 1830-2. It was built without scaffolding from the inside, floor by floor, with clay bricks baked nearby, and the sails were driven by an engine. It has now been restored to full working order and is open to visitors every Sunday in spring and summer.

The local historian, George Lipscomb, was born in Quainton in 1773 and lived at Magpie Cottage on the west side of the green. After studying medicine in London, he moved back to the village and began his *History of Antiquities of the County of Buckingham*. At first, he had a long list of subscribers backing him but gradually the cost of collating the material and travelling round the county used up his money. After the publication of the first volume, he continued writing in poverty and sadly his life ended in 1846 in the debtors' prison.

Today there is just one pub in the village – The George & Dragon – but before the Second World War there were seven pubs and the population was a lot less then! In those days too there were five grocers' shops, a draper's and three bakers. On Sundays, villagers would take their joints to the bakers in a baking tin with the Yorkshire pudding in a jug to be poured round the meat, and a tin of dripping for the roast potatoes. On Saturdays, their cakes would be baked for them and they could buy raw dough, take it home and work fruit, sugar and an egg into it to make dough cake.

One of the greatest local attractions is the Buckingshire Railway Centre, where visitors can take a ride in a restored steam train or on the model railway.

In earlier times, horse racing in the meadows adjacent to Strand (so named because the bustle of people was likened to the London Strand) was a local feature and a report of the races in August 1706 describes the large crowds arriving in every sort of conveyance. The green was covered with booths and there was a man in the stocks, covered with slime after a ducking in the nearby pond. Many of England's nobility were amongst the thousands gathered and Petty Constables were on the lookout for known pickpockets and troublemakers. It was hoped that Queen Anne would visit the races one day as she was rumoured to be interested in establishing a course at 'a place called Ascot'. The Winchendon Mile was the first race and the prize was a plate worth 50 guineas.

Today most of the villagers work either in Aylesbury or in and around the village, with a few commuting to London.

🍁 RADNAGE

The small village of Radnage is spread in and around the Chiltern Hills and has been settled for thousands of years by farming communities. The name Radnage seems to be derived from the Old English for 'Red Oak', although beech woods predominate in the area, with few oak trees. However, the Church of England school badge bears an oak leaf on a Cross of Lorraine. The double-barred Cross of Lorraine is also carved into the front door of St Mary's Church, thus bearing witness to the Knights Templar who farmed in the valley on their return from the Crusades.

Most of the village belonged to the Knights until their order was suppressed in the early 14th century. Since then, the land has passed to the Knights Hospitaller, the City of London and then back to the Crown.

A welcoming and caring community, we have a Winter Lunch Club for the over 65s, a Progressive Supper, a bi-annual Dinner & Dance, a Friendship Club, Garden Sunday, Snowdrop Sunday, the WI, and many other events. The doors to our beautiful 12th-century church are always open and we like to make everyone feel welcome.

Perched on a tranquil hilltop, Radnage seems to have its own little micro-climate – with the wind blowing at full pelt but also the chance to enjoy uninterrupted sunsets. The blanket of fog that occasionally sits over the valley between us and Bledlow Ridge can often make you feel like you're on top of a cloud, truly magical!

🍁 SANDS

Sands is a small community on the outskirts of High Wycombe – and it did not truly exist until 150 years ago. Up until then, there were just two farms, some farm cottages, a shooting lodge and a flax mill here, and all of these formed part of the West Wycombe Estate.

The name Sands originates from 'a lane to the sand pits', and refers to the lane which ran from West Wycombe Road to the sand pits on what is now Lane End Road. The first of the sand pits was located just past Newmer Common, where Lane End Road becomes Park Lane and crosses the M40 motorway; the second is now the shooting ground.

The entire lane was initially known as Sands Lane, but the first section was renamed Chapel Lane when the Chapel was constructed in the early 1900s. The sand pits were in operation up until the 1930s and young boys would play on the old rusty machinery and the rail tracks until they were finally closed and the site cleared. In the early 1940s, the Sands Women's Institute used to organise blackberry picking parties which would last for most of the day. A gathering of between 20 and 30 women along with their children would fill their willow baskets to the brim and return home with fingers black from the delicious juice.

Sands didn't really come into existence until a new road was built connecting the hamlet to Cressex. But after the First World War, Sands became a community in its own right. The residents applied to the war office and received an ex-army hut which became Sands War Memorial Hall. Just after the hut was erected, Saint Mary's Church was built alongside, a prefabricated building made from corrugated tin with a green bell on top.

Technically, it was at this time that Sands became a village since having its own church elevated it from simple hamlet status. However, there was still no mains water or sewerage system here until the 1930s.

Gallows Lane, which ran from Green Street to what is now Chapel Lane was not a popular place to live owing to the connotations of its name. So in 1938, St Mary and St George Church was built to replace St Mary's and the street name – at least the stretch of road where the church lay – was renamed Dashwood Avenue. Residents of four houses in what remains of Gallows Lane were furious when they found out the local council had changed the name of their street without telling them!

Up until the 1950s, the land between Pinewood Road and Hellbottom Wood was an open space for everyone. The area had been well known for butterflies, wild flowers and dog roses.

In the 1960s, further housing development including Combe Rise was started, and Sands Industrial Estate was built. This took away large parts of the remaining fields, only leaving land to the west which is now known as Sands Bank.

Sands Nature Reserve was set up in the early 1990s when Wycombe District Council leased the fields and woodlands north of Adams Park Football Ground to West Wycombe Estate and set the land aside as a place where nature could always thrive.

Seer Green & Jordans

Seer Green is a village in the Chiltern District of Buckinghamshire. It is in the Chiltern Hills between Beaconsfield and Chalfont St Giles.

The name Seer is derived from the Norman French for 'dry or arid place'. In manorial rolls of 1223 it was called La Sere. There is a local legend that the 'Seer' refers to Merlin, King Arthur's seer, who rested here on his journeys to and from Camelot.

Edward, the Black Prince, built a lodge here and he and his courtiers hunted deer in the surrounding forests. The lodge, now called Hall Place, still exists.

There is a map in the British Museum dated 1793 entitled 'The Hamlet of Seer Green, being part of the Manor of Farnham Royal in the county of Buckinghamshire belonging to the Hon Francis Godolphin Esq'. At that time there were about 16 houses and cottages, and the village boundaries remain the same today although the population, taken at the last census in 2011, is now over 2,300.

Some of the first Christians in Seer Green were the Baptists who originally held their meetings in private homes. In 1843, they formed a church which met in the present Parish Hall, which had been built to house a lacemaking school in 1829. Lacemaking was very prolific in the village at that time and the Seer Green pattern became the motif for many beautiful pieces of work.

The Church of England built the parish church in 1846 but Seer Green didn't become a separate parish until 1866. The village school opened in 1859 with Miss Emma Downes as headmistress. The original schoolroom is still in use today.

Seer Green did not at this time have mains water. In 1887, the Jubilee Well was built to mark the occasion of Queen Victoria's Golden Jubilee. The 140ft-deep public well was for the use of the whole village except on Sundays when it was kept locked. Village men used to meet for a smoke and chat whilst drawing their daily supplies.

In 1893, the Golden Jubilee of the founding of the Baptist Church saw the launch of fundraising for a new chapel. The foundation stone was laid on 15 August 1899, one of the stone layers being Mr Halford Mills – the father of Bertram Mills of circus fame. The Chapel opened on Easter Monday 1900 and people came from far and wide by horse or gig. There was no electricity in the village at that time, so the lighting was provided by paraffin oil lamps suspended from the ceiling.

Until the early part of the 20th century, Seer Green was mainly an agricultural village, known for its cherry orchards. The remnants of some of these orchards remain and in honour of this tradition the local school holds a Cherry Pie Fair every summer. In olden days, the village was a blaze of blossom and people came from far and wide to see it. Most cherries were sent to Covent Garden but there was plenty left to be baked into pies by the local baker Mr Lofty in his shop and the village became known as the Cherry Pie Village.

The first village post office was next door to the Baptist Chapel and just sold stamps. The post office moved several times and sadly has now closed, leaving the village without this facility.

Most of the older village shops that were scattered around the village have now also ceased trading but there is still a small number of shops including a grocer, butcher, hairdresser and even a dog grooming salon. There are still two pubs much used by villagers, The Jolly Cricketers and The Three Horseshoes.

The railway came to Seer Green in 1917, cutting right through the Du Pre estate and golf course at Wilton Park. Colonel Du Pre had the foresight to arrange for a halt to be built in Seer Green and at the same time expanded the 9-hole golf course in the grounds of Wilton Park to 18 holes with a new clubhouse beside the station halt. The halt was originally designed to serve the Golf Club not the villagers and at first there were only two trains a day. The Golf Club is still in existence and is now known as Beaconsfield Golf Club.

After the First World War, Seer Green House became a finishing school for debutantes including Princess Margarethe of Sweden and during the Second World War it became a convalescent home for wounded soldiers.

The poet Herbert Read lived in the village and wrote his poem *A War within a War* in Seer Green. TS Eliot often came to visit and his collection of poems which inspired the musical *Cats* was dedicated to Miss Susanna Morley, a Seer Green resident.

The new war memorial was dedicated in 2012, and is incredibly the first of its kind for the village.

Jordans village is immediately adjacent to Seer Green and is a centre for Quakerism. It is also the burial place of William Penn, the founder of Pennsylvania. Jordans village takes its name from Old Jordans, the farm where Quaker farmers lived in the 17th century and has one of the oldest Friends' Meeting Houses in the country. It was built in 1688 and the meeting rooms retain most of the original brick. Sadly it suffered a serious fire in 2005 when the modern extension was destroyed and the original room was severely damaged. Within the grounds of Old Jordans is the Mayflower Barn whose timbers are purported to have come from the Mayflower ship that carried the first pilgrims to America, although this cannot be proved. The Barn used to be open to the public and many visitors from all over the world came to see it but it is now in private hands and no longer open to the public.

🍁 SLAPTON

Slapton lies at the extreme eastern edge of the county, sandwiched between the River Ouzel, the county boundary, and the Grand Union Canal. The Saxon origin of the name means 'farm by a slippery place'. The incredibly heavy clay with which local gardeners have to grapple with is the result of glacial activity during the last Ice Age. Some residential properties have great views over to the glacial deposits of Ivinghoe Beacon and the eastern end of the Chilterns, which affords great opportunity for scenic walks. Slapton is on the Two Ridges Link path between the Greensand Ridge and the Beacon. The village as a whole has plenty of scope for off-road walking – perhaps this accounts for the significant dog population in the village!

Most dwellings in Slapton are clustered around a T-junction, on which stands the very picturesque Carpenters Arms, the second oldest building in the village, the oldest being the much-loved 13th-century church. The pub is an important meeting place for villagers in the absence of any school or shop. The compact nature of the village may be responsible for the great community spirit which exists in Slapton. The village boasts an active church congregation as well as a large number of organisations: cycling clubs, drama group, thriving WI, craft club & book group. Many of these groups rely on the village hall, which has an active management committee. They are responsible for organising the annual village fete, an important event in the village calendar.

As mentioned, the church is the oldest building in the village. Its foundations date back to the 8th century and Saxon times. In recent years, the church has undergone extensive external restoration and the limewash used on the exterior means it can be spotted easily from the Chilterns Hills, even though the tower's diminutive height means it is dwarfed by adjoining conifers. Notable among its incumbents has been Rev John Kempe, who was vicar here in the early 1400s and then named Archbishop of Canterbury from 1452-1454. At the Christmas Eve service there is always standing room only at the church for later arrivals as many of the villagers make this a traditional start to their Christmas.

The proximity to the canal has also had an impact on the village. In earlier times, when much cargo was carried on horse-drawn narrowboats, the village provided rest and refreshment for the horses. The old site of

Church Farm, now demolished, provided stabling and a large pond which attracted the horsemen, as the water could be used to soothe the horses' hooves. Nowadays, traffic on the canal is almost entirely recreational and many anglers enjoy the tranquility of its banks and the possibility of catching 30lbs-plus carp.

Although many villagers work outside the village, there are now employment opportunities within the village, particularly at the equestrian enterprise at Bury Farm. This attracts equestrians from far afield as it is the venue for some national competitions. Another recent development has been the provision of luxury wigwams for 'glamping' stays on a farm site adjacent to the canal; the views from this site across to the Chilterns must be some of the best for miles around.

While something of a country idyll, the village nevertheless has had its moments of notoriety. The bridge where the Great Train Robbery took place in August 1963 is on the western edge of the village.

The Slapton parish council also manages the affairs of the two local hamlets of Grove and Horton. A marina has been developed at Grove Lock to cater for the increased demand for moorings.

Mention of Grove leads on to Slapton parish's most significant royal link. In May 1480, the abbey there was leased to one Lady Cicely Neville, mother of King Edward IV. She held this estate for the next 15 years until her death. Horton has its own much more recent notable connections as the home of Mr Shand Kydd, close friend and brother-in-law of Lord Lucan. On the eve of his disappearance, Lucan asked Kydd if he would assume responsibility for the three Lucan children, who in due course, were adopted by Kydd and spent time at Horton Hall. Kydd quipped that he bought the hall on the profits from Polyfilla, marketed by his family.

🍁 SPEEN

The village of Speen lies in the Chiltern Hills in the parish of Lacey Green and Loosley Row. At the time of the Domesday Book there were only a handful of dwellings in the area, but the 16th-18th centuries saw many more houses and inns built. Many of the houses are still inhabited today, but unfortunately all the inns have since closed for business.

In the past, Speen was a fairly closed community with many cottage industries and small holdings. The most famous occupations were 'bodging' to make chair legs for the furniture industry in High Wycombe and lacemaking, which the girls learned at a very early age. These are now hobbies rather than employment but the crafts live on. These days there are still many entrepreneurs working from home in the village, but many commute to neighbouring towns or into London.

There is a wonderful village shop and post office which was opened as part of a small housing development in 1998. Other significant buildings in the village include the Village Hall. Originally built in 1874 as a Temperance Hall, it was bought by the village in 1924. Over the years it has been improved and extended and now provides a home for the Pre-School, the WI, a bridge club, a pop-up pub and many one-off village events. The Village School, C of E voluntary aided, thrives in its 1966 building which replaced the original schoolhouse built in 1860.

Although the parish church is in Lacey Green, the Baptist chapel, which was built from local brick and flint in 1802, is still used as a regular place of worship. It has recently had a very sympathetic new extension housing a light and airy meeting room which also acts as a community hub and a café on a regular weekly basis. A walk around its churchyard not only reveals the identity of villagers over the two centuries, but also the grave of Eric Gill, the famous stone carver and designer.

Speen residents are fortunate to have a large open space – the playing fields – in the centre of the village, thanks to villagers who bought the land in 1935 for the sum of £160. This is managed by a playing fields committee and all are welcome to use the tennis court and children's play area here. Every year, it is home to the Family Fun Day in June and a huge bonfire and firework display on the weekend nearest to 5 November.

In July, the playing fields also host the annual Village Fete. All the village organisations contribute to the planning and running of the stalls and sideshows with all the villagers joining in on the day. It raises valuable funds to help maintain all the activities that happen in this small but vibrant community.

Every two years, Speen hosts a week-long Festival based in a marquee on the field. This also brings everyone together with a drama or musical production featuring local residents, art exhibition, lectures and outdoor events – and it is well supported by residents and visitors alike.

As well as its beautiful situation and lovely old buildings, it is this sense of community that makes Speen a special place.

🍁 STEWKLEY

Stewkley, originally a linear village in the Aylesbury Vale District. is renowned for being the longest village in England. The name Stewkley is derived from Old English for 'a woodland clearing with tree stumps' and is recorded in the Domesday Book of 1086 as 'Stiuclai'.

The village is situated along the watershed between the Rivers Thames and Ouse and includes the hamlets of North End and Stewkley Dean. It is 4 miles north of Leighton Buzzard and 5 miles east of Winslow, with a population of about 1,900 in 752 households.

Stewkley came to fame in the early 1970s as villagers fought to save it from destruction to make way for the building of London's third airport. Stewkley was saved by a vigorous campaign conducted by the villagers and notable locals such as Sir Evelyn de Rothschild, Sir Desmond Fennell, a barrister living in Winslow, and Peter Warner, who set up Wing Resistance Association to fight the proposal. The parish church of St Michael and All Angels is one of the least altered of England's Norman churches, a remarkable example of Romanesque style, and there is also a handsome Methodist Chapel. It was the preservation of the church and the lack of suitable property to re-home long-standing village families that saved Stewkley from destruction. This victory is commemorated by the Airport Monument (in the shape of Concorde) and Spinney.

Stewkley developed, and while it is still an agricultural area, its history includes trades such as blacksmiths, wheelwrights and saddle makers. Lacemaking and straw plaiting were also common until the 1850s. The local clay was fired in Stewkley and examples of this can be seen in early chapel buildings and the National School, built in 1860, opposite the church, in High Street North. Permission for the National School to be built was granted in 1860 and the running of the school was to be the responsibility of the vicar, church wardens and two parishioners.

The well-kept recreation ground leads to a unique wild flower reserve which is lovingly tended and provides a valuable village resource. The recreation ground also has cricket and football pitches and a high standard is achieved by teams in local leagues. A group of parents also run regular weekend training sessions open to all village children. Two excellent tennis courts, an enclosed kick-ball area and adult outdoor gym equipment are also available and benefit from flood lights when required. A new Scout hut was built in 2019. The refurbished pavilion is used to provide facilities for all sports teams and is also a venue for a local GP's surgery as well as a base for youth organisations and other village activities.

Stewkley Village Hall, which was opened in 1925, was refurbished in 2008 when the kitchen facilities and entrance hall were modernised. This makes it suitable for many varied functions. The hall is used by numerous local groups such as badminton, drama, indoor bowls and the

The parish church of St Michael and All Angels. Stewkley

WI, as well as for Parish Council meetings. The School Room in the Methodist Church is used for lunches and a toddlers' group.

A monthly newsletter, the *Stewkley Grapevine*, is produced, edited and delivered by volunteers to all houses in Stewkley Parish. The *Grapevine* keeps villagers up to date with all events and local news, as well as providing a valuable service detailing local tradespeople.

The War Memorial, tended by committed volunteers, stands at the junction of three roads and is the focal point of the annual Armistice Service organised by the local British Legion. Volunteers also keep the whole village free from litter and provide and maintain floral displays, enabling Stewkley to win the Best Kept Village in its category.

Well-known names associated with the village include Al Murray (comedian), Alastair Cook and Darren Gough (cricketers) and Emmeline Pankhurst (suffragette), the Earl and Countess of Orkney, as well as an alleged ghost of Reverend William Wadley who had a long-flowing beard, riding a white horse!

The gradual development of Stewkley is shown by the differing styles of architecture from thatched cottages to present-day dwellings. The two Methodist Chapels did not amalgamate until 1987 when the last service was held in Chapel Square. The local primary school, St Michael's C of E School which takes pupils aged from four to eleven, relocated to modern facilities in Chapel Square in 1977. The Stewkley Cygnets pre-school group, which received an outstanding Ofsted report, is also based there. At one time the village had numerous shops and pubs but is now served by just two pubs, The Swan and The Carpenter's Arms. The shop, which is situated in High Street North, is very well stocked to cater for local needs.

Stewkley today is a thriving rural community with opportunities for all ages, and there are also several small businesses within the parish. It is within striking distance of Milton Keynes with all the facilities that an urban area provides, as well as being an easy commute to work in a number of directions including Birmingham and London.

🍁 STOKE MANDEVILLE

Stoke Mandeville is a village and civil parish in the Vale of Aylesbury, three miles from the town centre. There are three pubs – The Bull (1793), The Bell (1798) and The Woolpack which at one time incorporated the smithy (1756). There is a shop/post office, excellent schools, as well as the parish church of St Mary the Virgin and a Methodist church. The Ark, on the Risborouqh Road, is the church office as well as a place for informal meetings and coffee mornings. The Ark is built on the site of the old National School, which was opened in 1843.

The village is mentioned in the Domesday Book (1086) when it was listed as 'Stoches', the Mandeville part was first used when Geoffrey de Mandeville first held the manor. The name Stoke Mandeville is known around the world due to the hospital, originally built outside the village after a severe cholera epidemic in the 1830s. It is now renowned as a world centre for spinal injuries, and where the first paralympics took place in 1948.

A great place for families to visit is The Buck Goat Centre, an open farm in the village where visitors can pet and feed the goats. There is also an art gallery and other businesses within the vicinity.

Stoke Mandeville WI is a small friendly group, which was set up in 1926 and which is fortunate to benefit from a grant donated by the Stoke Mandeville and Other Parishes Charity. This charity was set up in 1986 following some extensive local research into the ownership of some land and a gravel pit at Prestwood. It came to light that this land was in fact owned by Stoke Mandeville Parish Council who subsequently sold some of it, investing the money for the charity to spend on the inhabitants of the three local parishes.

There are a number of interesting old houses, some dating from the 15th century, for example the cottage next to the Bull inn bears the date 1409.

Stoke Mandeville is still a pleasant place to live, much changed from the original rural community dependent on farms for work; today there is increased housing development resulting in more traffic and ongoing concerns about the construction of the HS2 rail line. So more changes to come, but Stoke Mandeville village will survive, as it has in the past. The Village Community Centre, built in 1977 with excellent facilities, is host to many activities, and is where our WI meetings are held every month.

🍁 STOKE POGES

On the southern tip of Buckinghamshire, Stoke Poges is a semi-rural area just three miles from Slough, with easy connections to London.

The village is an old established parish and is mentioned in the Domesday Book.

Close to the church are the Stoke Poges Memorial Gardens, set in twenty acres of formal gardens and landscaping. In 1935, the Mobbs family bought the land here to protect the area from being built upon. Beautifully kept up by experts and volunteers, the Grade II listed gardens were placed on Historic England's Register of Parks and Gardens in 1996.

Nearby is Stoke Park, home to the 16th-century Manor House. In 1596, Sir Edward Coke became the manor's owner and entertained Queen Elizabeth here in 1601. He was a very influential lawyer who became Lord Chief Justice and petitioned for a law replacing powers from the King to Parliament. In 1800, a tall monument to Sir Edward Coke was erected in the grounds of Stoke Park which still stands.

Later, in the 18th century, the Penn family (who founded the Colony of Pennsylvania) came to live in the Manor House. John Penn decided to build a replacement, and a new mansion was built in the middle of the park which stands to this day. The mansion has changed hands many times but has now been restored and is a luxury hotel with an 18-hole golf course.

The poet, Thomas Gray, wrote *Elegy Written in a Country Churchyard* about St Giles' Church, whilst living in Stoke Poges. He is buried in the churchyard and on land nearby is a large monument in his honour with verses from the poem carved in stone.

With the break-up of the great estates, formation of the modern village began. Stoke Poges is now a parish of some 5,000 inhabitants and, unlike some villages, is thriving. Stoke Poges is extremely fortunate in being a village with enough shops to supply everyday needs, including a post office and a chemist. There is also a doctors' surgery. The Parish Council does an excellent job and the Recreation Ground, which comes under their care, provides facilities for football, tennis, adult exercise equipment plus a children's play area. A 500m running track has recently been installed. The local allotments are also well used and loved.

To the north of the village lies Stoke Common. This is a large area of heathland crossed by public footpaths and is a 'Site of Special Scientific Interest' due to the 26 rare or special species of plants growing there. Rare breeds of cattle graze on the common in the summer and volunteers from the village work hard to maintain this natural habitat for all the plants and small animals.

Three organisations within the village have survived over 100 years, namely The Horticultural Society, The Women's Institute and, what is now called, The Village Centre.

The WI was founded in 1919 and still meets monthly with a full programme. Many friendships are formed there. The Horticultural Society is 125 years old and organises a flower and produce show every year. The marquee is filled with flowers, vegetables, jams and cakes – the competition is fierce! A recent addition has been the interest shown by the Society in local schools resulting in excellent and original entries in the children's section. The grounds are covered with various stalls and a brass band plays throughout the afternoon.

The Village Hall has stood on the site in Rogers Lane for over 100 years. Following recent refurbishment and additions it was re-named 'The Village Centre'. It is the hub of many village activities from classes to plays and weddings. The Social Club is there also and is a great meeting place for villagers. The Stoke Poges Players, an amateur dramatic society, present a summer play and always an uproarious Christmas pantomime. The Stoke Poges Singers give concerts which are well attended.

There are several events which have become village traditions along with the pantomime. There is a village fete and the outdoor 'Carols on the Green'. The latter is further enhanced by the Christmas lights provided by the Parish Council.

The youth of the village are not forgotten. There are active Air Scouts, Brownies, Guides and the opportunity to train for the Duke of Edinburgh Awards. Three nursery schools thrive and are always full of happy children. The local primary school is very active and has an excellent reputation.

A sister church to St Giles' is St Andrew's, well loved by young families for its lively outlook. It sports an attractive coffee shop, run by volunteers, which is always warm and welcoming and holds a weekly 'Knit & Natter' group.

The Village Green has been greatly improved by the addition of boxes of flowers and spring bulbs. The very latest addition is the 'Spirit of Peace' statue, fashioned mainly out of scrap metal, cutlery, saucepans etc, much of which was donated by villagers who had connections to the World Wars.

There is much to offer in the village, contributing to the feeling of belonging that many people experience. This is due in no small part to the willingness to volunteer to help with all the activities. Stoke Poges is a great place to live.

🍁 STOKENCHURCH

Stokenchurch is a hill-top village in the Chilterns on the A40 between London and Oxford. It is also on Junction 5 of the M40 above the steep chalk cutting rising up from the Oxfordshire plain, with red kites circling overhead. In the Domesday Book of 1086, Stokenchurch was an upland settlement in the large parish of Aston Rowant, Oxfordshire, used for grazing and firewood. Its name may derive from 'church made of wood', 'stoke' or 'stock' meaning timber. Alternatively it may come from 'stocc' meaning an outlying farm or secondary settlement with the addition of 'church' when the present St Peter and St Paul Church was first built in the 12th century. The village became part of Buckinghamshire in 1896.

Besides the parish church, there has been a strong tradition of Methodism in the village. Hannah Ball, the founder of Sunday schools, was born and buried here. The surviving Methodist chapel is late Victorian and one of the most elaborate in Buckinghamshire. There was also a Congregational church.

Stokenchurch folk have a tradition for being independently minded. This may be due to the relatively harsh climate, poor soil or lack of natural water resources they had to overcome, but one thing they *did* have were the magnificent woods of beech with ash and elm. This gave rise to a flourishing furniture industry. Walking through the woods today, you can still see the man-made pits where logs were cut into planks, one man at the top with the saw and the other in the pit below in all the dust; hence the sayings 'top dog' and 'under-dog'. 'Bodgers' lived in the woods turning the pole lathes to make chair legs and other parts, and also charcoal burners, giving rise to the name of Colliers Lane, part of a trackway to the north of the parish. This was mainly used by drovers and pack animals but also by some travellers who might have preferred to avoid the village since Stokenchurch, like many remote Chiltern villages, had a reputation for crime and lawlessness.

Timber auctions were held in late autumn at The Kings Arms. Catalogues were sent out but with very few details of where each lot was to be found so the buyer had to track them down himself to assess them. This involved finding the woodman in charge of each wood, often by visiting the many public houses in the area. Timber viewings would often turn into a very pleasant if hazy afternoon! Stokenchurch is lucky to have several areas of common land in the centre of the village. They had been set aside for exercise and recreation for the villagers after the Enclosure Award for Stokenchurch was agreed in 1861. There was also to be a Horse Fair and Fun Fair, with horses arriving from very early in the morning and travellers, farmers and dealers on hand to do their deals outside one of the many public houses.

Allotments and the cricket ground occupy some of the area today. It is also used for the summer fete, a visiting funfair and circus, and an open air church service. In 1951, the Parish Council bought the commons when offered them by Colonel Clerke-Brown, the Lord of the Manor. Hopefully they will remain open spaces, forever reminding us of the landscape of the Domesday Book and earlier.

Elizabeth I passed through Stokenchurch on her way to Rycote and in March 1680 Charles II stayed at the George Inn with Queen Catherine. Apparently she was accommodated in a tent on the common while one of the King's mistresses, possibly Nell Gwynne, was admitted to his apartment. The George was built in the 16th century and is now the Kings Hotel, having been the Kings Arms for many years. During the Civil War, several skirmishes were fought in and around Stokenchurch. The villagers were generally thought to be for Parliament but most of the church plate was melted down in the King's cause. Adrian Scrope of Wormsley signed the death warrant for Charles I and was himself executed after the Restoration. The Wormsley estate, part of which is in the parish of Stokenchurch, was sold to Mr J P Getty Jr in 1984. It now hosts the Garsington opera company for a seven-week period every summer, and celebrity cricket matches to which villagers have been invited.

One of the few listed buildings in Stokenchurch is Tippings, a fine 17th-century house. It was built by Bartholomew Tipping and included the foundation of a school for the education of 12 poor boys of the parish. It opened in 1676 and continued for the next 250 years. When it finally closed in 1935, a charity was set up with the trust's money to help Stokenchurch children with their education.

Since the 1960s, the village population has grown to 4,810 (2011) with several new housing estates and schools being built. The M40 was eventually extended to Birmingham which improved Stokenchurch's links with the rest of the country via the motorway system. The secondary school and two banks have gone but the medical centre, post office and library, now run by volunteers, survive. It may have become a commuter village to some extent but a community spirit still thrives with small businesses and many varied village activities.

🍁 STONY STRATFORD

Stony Stratford is a much-loved town within Milton Keynes which dates back to Roman times. Watling Street, one of five ancient roads that traversed Britain, forded the River Ouse here. That gave the town its name: 'Stratford' means 'ford on a Roman road' and 'Stony' refers to the stones on the bed of the ford.

Officially made a town in 1215, Stony Stratford has several links to medieval royalty.

In 1290, the funeral cortege of Queen Eleanor of Castile stopped in Stony Stratford overnight on its way to London. An Eleanor cross to mark the route was erected but was then destroyed during the English Civil War, although we still have a Queen Eleanor Street to this day.

And recently Luke McDonnell painted a beautiful mural of Queen Eleanor on the side of the cycle shop.

The boy-king Edward V is alleged to have stayed at the former Rose & Crown Inn here in 1483 before heading to London – where he would later mysteriously die with his young brother (the Two Princes) in the Tower.

Perhaps most famously, Stony Stratford is said to be the birthplace of the phrase 'cock and bull story'. The saying is believed to refer to stagecoach travellers' gossip exchanged between two coaching inns on the High Street here. The Cock and The Bull (both still in existence) were a main stopping point on the turnpike road from London to Chester and North Wales.

Of course, things have changed since those days. How very quiet it was before the A5 was built and you could hear the sound of sheep grazing on nearby farms from Queen Eleanor Street.

The High Street offers much, including a coffee shop, newsagents, hairdressers and a supermarket – but without the variety of shops and facilities we once had.

Now gone but missed, we had a tannery with links to India, a haberdasher's, a shoe shop, a bus garage and even a cinema, unusual for a little town like ours.

But people still love our town, and it has been used many times as a film location. *Withnail And I* was shot in Stony, with one shop in Market Square turned into a café for several scenes.

Stony Stratford has a colourful history, but nowadays the colours which most visitors to the town notice are the flowers. There are flowers in planters on every corner, in window boxes and hanging baskets and in flower beds around the town. They are tended by a dedicated band of 50 volunteers and we have won many Britain in Bloom Gold awards, as well as Buckinghamshire Best Kept Village Competition.

We are all rightly proud of Stony Stratford, and anybody who says otherwise is telling you a cock and bull story!

Let's take a walk through the town where I live,
And see places of interest and the joy that they give.
We'll start where the gas works was (not there any more).
No need for it now there's North Sea gas galore.

We pass by the place where Queen Eleanor rested,
Just a plaque on the wall now where martins have nested.
The road widens out where the cross used to be,
and it would still be there but for Oliver C.

There's an old ruined church that's just left to rot,
Surrounded by gravestones of folk long forgot.
They won't pull it down so there's no need for qualms,
It's emblazoned upon the town's coat of arms.

The Cock and the Bull in the middle of town
Are next to each other and are pubs of renown.
Where people thought up tales to get the most glory.
From one pub to the other, hence a "Cock and Bull story".

Let's walk up the path where the faithful have trod,
The people that need to be near their God.
We stop to look up to the top of the tower
Where the church bell is ringing to quarter the hour.

We pass by the church and enter the square
Where a long time ago people peddled their ware.
Now cars are parked in allotted spaces,
Where horses once patiently stood in their traces.

We stand by the tree sadly not quite as tall
As when John Wesley preached his new method to all.
Some vandals once tried to set it alight,
but it still struggles on, it won't give up the fight.

Turning the corner we come onto the green,
Where the biggest horse fair in the country had been.
They say it was the best in the land
Where a horse could be bought with a shake of the hand.

There's a plaque on a building that tells of the pity
Of two boys who stayed on the way to the city.
One of the boys was destined to be King,
Until Richard Plantagenet took them under his wing.

If I could live anywhere I choose.
I would still wish to live in the town by the Ouse.
Knowing the rest of my life would be spent
In a town where the people are truly content.

TAPLOW & HITCHAM

Picturesque Taplow village has a population of approximately 2,000. The village has one pub, the Oak & Saw, a hotel, St Nicolas Church and Village Hall together with C of E first and middle schools. On the edge of the parish was the notorious Skindles Hotel which has been demolished and is now a Roux Brothers bistro. The village is often used as a location for TV and film, with appearances in *The Vicar of Dibley* and *Midsomer Murders*. Taplow railway station is close by and is linked to Maidenhead via Isambard Kingdom Brunel's 1838 bridge, which continues to carry trains 180 years later. The two arches are reported to be the widest and flattest in the world. A clap of the hands or a call within the sounding arches produces an amazing echo.

There is evidence of occupation in the village that goes back 1,300 years. Within the grounds of Taplow Court can be found Taeppa's Low, a Saxon burial mound which was excavated in 1883. Traces of the body of Taeppa, thought to be a prince or chieftain, were discovered within an oak-lined burial chamber, clad in gold embroidered robes and accompanied by an astounding collection of grave goods. This lavishly equipped burial was the richest find of the period in England until the discovery of the Sutton Hoo treasure in 1939, and it remains one of the finest known examples of its class. The artefacts are now on display in the British Museum.

Taplow Court has a long history and it is said that a young Elizabeth I was kept prisoner there during the reign of her sister, Mary. Probably the most prominent family to have occupied the house is the Grenfells. Lord Desborough, William Grenfell, moved there from Taplow House and he was the chairman of the Olympic Association responsible for bringing the 1908 Olympics to London. He was an Olympic fencer, ran and rowed for Oxford, swam across the Niagara twice and climbed the Matterhorn three times.

Taplow Court is now occupied by SGI UK, a Buddhist movement that follows the teachings of a 13th-century Japanese sage. They welcome visitors to view the house and grounds some weekends in the summer.

Taplow House is a beautiful Georgian building with six acres of landscaped gardens, and is now a four-star hotel. Audrey Skimming, whose family lived there, founded Taplow and Hitcham WI at the request of Nancy Astor who (along with her niece, Joyce Grenfell) was an active member of Cliveden and Dropmore WI.

Close by Taplow village is the spectacular house and estate of Cliveden, originally built by George Villiers, the second Duke of Buckingham, in the 1660s. It is thought he built the house for his mistress, the Countess of Shrewsbury. On hearing of the affair, her husband challenged Buckingham to a duel and was killed. The present house is the third to be built here, as the others burned down.

In 1893, Nancy and Waldorf Astor purchased the estate and it was once again the centre for lavish hospitality and famous guests – George Bernard Shaw, Gandhi, Winston Churchill, Laurence Olivier and Vivien Leigh to name but a few. Nancy Astor was to become the first woman to sit as an MP in the House of Commons.

Cliveden hit the headlines in 1963 when it became known that John Profumo, Secretary of State for War, had been introduced to Christine Keeler here while she may have been in a relationship with a Russian spy. It was the end of his career and nearly brought down the Conservative government.

Hitcham, a small village linking Taplow with Burnham, is mentioned in the Domesday Book when thirteen families resided there. The ancient church of St Mary's dates from 1126. The civil parish of Hitcham was abolished in 1934 and was divided up between Burnham, Taplow and Dorney.

A large area of Hitcham around the church, including the old manor site, was bought in 1864 by George Hanbury, a brewer and hop merchant. He built Hitcham House which is now Grade II listed although there had been a house on the estate since the 17th century which Elizabeth I visited in 1602. It was used as a nurses' home for staff working at the Canadian Red Cross Memorial Hospital in Cliveden. Now it has been divided into several residential properties.

Nashdom (meaning 'our home' in Russian) Abbey to the north of the parish has also been converted to apartments. This country house was designed by Edwin Lutyens in 1907-8 for Prince Alexis Dolgorouki and his wife. They are both now buried in St Mary's churchyard. From 1924 until 1997 it was home for an order of Anglican Benedictine monks. Probably the most famous resident of Hitcham was Sir Terry Wogan.

Taplow and Hitcham WI is privileged to have its own Hall thanks to some great fundraising efforts by members in the 1920s and a donation by Lord Desborough's daughter of some additional land. It has an interesting history – during the war it was used as a reception centre for evacuees with families sleeping on the floor until homes could be found. Ration books were issued from here. Members ran a mobile canteen servicing Army camps and the local Prisoner of War Camp on the field next door. There was a library in one of the rooms and for many years a weekly child clinic was manned by WI members. Today, the Hall still hosts many community activities and events.

🍁 TERRIERS

Lying on the northern edge of High Wycombe and straddling the A404 as it leads to Amersham is Terriers.

Its name owes nothing to dogs but probably derives from a personal name or the nickname of a man who tarried or delayed. The spelling has changed over the years; in 1714 it was Tarryers but it has also been variously known as Tayers and Taryers.

Since the mid-18th century there have been many boundary changes, both civil and ecclesiastical. As a result, the line between Terriers and the contiguous Totteridge (Tutterige in 1179 and subsequently Tota's Ridge or Look-out Hill) has become blurred and the two areas are frequently referred to as one. By 1927 however, Terriers (and Totteridge) had been absorbed into the municipality of High Wycombe.

Historically an area of farms with a few houses dotted about, major changes began in 1921 when the first council houses were built along with the development of an urban road system, leading to some ribbon development. These changes have continued to the present day, resulting in the densely populated residential area it now is.

The road to Amersham too has seen changes. Until 1881 it was a toll road with a toll house at what is now Terriers crossroads. Originally the toll gate (without a house) was at Hazlemere but it was moved in 1829 to its last site at Terriers. In 1881 two toll houses, Terriers and that of the Wycombe Hill toll, were sold for £120. The house was demolished in 1970, being replaced by two shops. The site has been further developed and is now a restaurant and a taxi hire office.

Although Terriers cannot boast a clearly identifiable centre it does have three buildings of note. The most prominent, sited as it is atop Amersham Hill, is the Anglican Church of St Francis of Assisi. It was built largely because of the determination of the Reverend Frederick Field and his wife Henrietta. Having worked in the diocese they felt that Terriers should have its own church and pledged money to support the living. After further fundraising the proposal was agreed and the famed architect Sir Giles Gilbert Scott was commissioned to draw up plans. Building was rapid and on 11 October 1930 the completed church was consecrated. It was not, however, until 1937 that a new parish was formally recognised. When built it stood alone, still surrounded by fields, a huge, unmissable building. To this day, now in the midst of urban development it still stands out especially when viewed from lower down in the town.

Almost opposite the church is the Royal Grammar School whose history goes back to the 16th century. As a result of the Reformation, the ancient Hospital of St John the Baptist, the ruins of which are still to be seen in the town, ceased to exist and its funds were put to education. Originally in Eastern Street, by the late 19th century the school had more than outgrown its premises. Land at the top of Amersham Hill was purchased and in February 1914, building began to a design by Arthur Vernon. On 15 July 1915, the school moved to its new home and has gone from strength to strength. Buildings have been added, particularly its new frontage in 1962. Proximity to the school causes Terriers to be popular with house buyers.

The third prominent building is Terriers House on the A404. A Georgian house of the mid-18th century, for most of its life it has been a family home, but for some time it has housed the headquarters of an international company.

Although not so well known, Magdala House is also of interest – as it was the birthplace in 1882 of Geoffrey (later Sir Geoffrey) de Havilland. After building his first plane in 1908, he went on to lead the company bearing his name and which produced such iconic aircraft as the Tiger Moth, the Mosquito and, in 1952 the Comet, the world's first jet passenger airliner. His father had been a curate at Holy Trinity church in Hazlemere and when Geoffrey was two the family moved away. Research has shown that Magdala House is now Terriers Green House and in July 2000 a plaque commemorating its famous son was fixed to the building.

During the Second World War, High Wycombe was involved with aircraft manufacture. Although none of the work was undertaken in Terriers, the area did not escape direct contact with the war. In 1944, a V-1 rocket (a 'doodlebug') landed on what was then open ground near to the church. There was some damage to property but no injuries. Had it happened today…

The part of Totteridge Common which reaches up to the A404 lends itself to being regarded as Terriers's village green. A pleasant, grassy area with trees, it is popular with walkers, many with a wide variety of dogs. And so, although its name does not refer to dogs, Terriers may be said to live up to it.

🍁 THE LEE & LEE COMMON

Set high in the Chiltern Hills you will find, clustered around a quintessentially English village green, the village of The Lee, with its pub, manor house and cottages built in the Arts and Crafts style by the Liberty family, of Regent Street store fame.

Sir Arthur Lasenby Liberty bought the Manor and estate in 1898 and the family's connection with the village continues today. As you approach the village from the direction of Great Missenden, the figurehead of Admiral Lord Howe stares out at you from the driveway of 'Pipers'.

It is from HMS *Impregnable*, the last wooden-hulled warship built for the Royal Navy. Sir Arthur obtained the ship's timbers when it was decommissioned and scrapped, using them on the facade of his London store. The figurehead is Grade II listed.

Just north-west of the green lies the original site of Lee, a woodland clearing with an Iron Age fort. Walk into it past the 'new' church (built in the 1860s) and you will find the old church dating from about 1220. Outside see the mass clocks, sundials for telling the time for mass and the unusual wooden gravestones; inside see mediaeval wall paintings and the only known stained-glass window depicting Oliver Cromwell. Come on a summer Sunday afternoon and you will find the villagers and visitors gathered there for cream teas.

Back past the Manor you will find the cricket ground in The Lee Manor Park. Cricket was a part of the house parties at the Manor in the early 20th century and in August 1914, a match between the Manor and the villagers was abandoned due to rain just as the First World War was declared. Almost all the eligible men joined up to fight for their country and the cricketers vowed to complete the match after fighting ended. But the village lost 30 men, and 36 were wounded, mainly at the Battle of Fromelles in July 1916. Almost every family in the village was affected and the loss is still felt to this day. Their names are on the memorial you can see on the village green. In 2014, teams representing the village and the Manor finally completed the match as a tribute to those who gave their lives for us. The Manor team won by 11 runs! The town of Fromelles in northern France and The Lee village now share many close ties. If you walk up the lane opposite The Cock & Rabbit pub to Field End you will find a seat which looks over farmland where it is said the women and girls of the village said goodbye to their menfolk and watched as they walked off to war, many never to return.

Come to the park on the third Saturday in July each year to experience a wonderful local tradition, The Lee Flower Show. The Show is not just a horticultural event though, but a vibrant village fete with a local arts and crafts display, sports, a dog show, stalls and games of all kinds, and famed for its home-made teas. The Show has its origins in the Liberty tradition, begun in 1892, of inviting staff from London for a country picnic.

Across the park, walking up past the village school, you will find Oxford Street (no, not that one) which used to have a village shop owned by a local man named John Lewis!

Along Oxford Street is the Jubilee well, dug originally in 1897, the year of Queen Victoria's Diamond Jubilee. It is 365 feet deep and when in use there were two counteracting buckets each holding 25 gallons of water. Used until the 1950s, it is now a listed building.

The Methodist Chapel is a reminder of the village's non-conformist tradition. Built by local people as a primitive Methodist Church in the 1830s, it was a school in the 1840s and 50s and continues as the oldest Methodist Church in the Amersham Circuit. Round the corner in Lee Clump you can see what used to be a Strict Baptist Chapel (now a farm) with the gravestones in its garden. James 'Holy Jim' Pearce is still famous for his preaching and writing, full of religious fire.

This is a lively village with lots going on. We have two pubs, The Cock & Rabbit on The Lee green and The Old Swan in the neighbouring hamlet of Swan Bottom (where a Bronze Age gold bracelet, now in Aylesbury Museum, was found). We have a Parish Hall with a tennis court, which hosts activities like wine tasting,

The Lee school

Pilates, evening classes and a nursery school. Alongside that, we have a vibrant community shop, staffed by volunteers, and our Scout Hut where the Scouts, Cubs and Beavers often depart for outings in their vintage bus.

Of course if you come to visit us beware – it is a dangerous place as one of the locations used in the BBC's *Midsomer Murders* series.

THORNBOROUGH & THORNTON

'A hill where thorn trees grow' aka Thornborough and 'Thorn tree by a farm' aka Thornton are villages whose roots (and presumably thorns) stretch back far into the mists of time, back to the Domesday Book of 1086 for certain. In Thornborough's case, the Roman earthworks on its western border and two Roman mounds (tumuli) are clear evidence of a community dating back even further.

Bishop Kennet, writing in 1695, recorded that there may have been a battle on Thornborough Bridge against the Roman army. The bridge – which actually dates back to the 14th century – is the only surviving medieval bridge in the county. We are very proud of our bridge and also the tumuli, even though when they were excavated in 1839, they contained meagre pickings: a few pottery vessels and bits of glass.

Thornton also has evidence of Roman workings in the form of a wharf on the River Ouse. It is recorded that in Roman times, there were wharves approximately every three miles that were used for collecting grain from the local areas, resulting in the overall area sometimes being described as the 'bread basket' of the Roman army.

In the centre of Thornborough village, between the 17th-century manor, the village hall and the village school, stands St Mary's Church. Parts of the south wall are believed to date from Saxon times, but the earliest records begin in the 12th century. The church tower houses a peal of five steel bells, which were re-hung in 1986 after a silence of thirty years.

It is thought that St Michael & All Angels' Church in Thornton dates from 1219, though it was dramatically restored in the late 18th century. It too has a bell tower and once had a working clock created by E. Dent & Co. London, although the clock face and mechanisms await funding for restoration. There are other Dent clocks in St Pancras station (a reproduction of the original) and in the Elizabeth Tower surrounding Big Ben.

Essentially, in times gone by, both of these villages were communities characterised by manual labour or specialised trades. Occupations listed in the 1851 census for Thornborough include baker, grocer, butcher, wheelwright, tailor, stonemason, innkeeper, boot and shoemaker, carpenter, blacksmith, carter, vicar, teacher, pillow and lace makers and servants. Thornton, the smaller of the two, had named occupations of agricultural labourer, architect, brush maker, bailiff, carpenter, gamekeeper and governess.

Nowadays, the old farmhouses and labourers' cottages in Thornborough have been renovated into desirable residences – attracting buyers from professional families and well-paid commuters. Clearly, modernity has brought many changes to village life but both parishes are alive and well.

Whilst there is no longer a shop or a butcher in Thornborough village and only one pub, there is still a thriving village infant school and separate pre-school, church and chapel services and events, a Woodland Trust, an active Thornborough and Thornton WI, a Cricket Club, Sports Club and Social Club. The Village Hall is used for numerous events, parties and meetings – we have a Thornborough and Thornton Horticultural Society, a Thornborough and Thornton Fundraising Committee, a Fun Run, Bonfire Night, Harvest Supper and Merry Christmas Market every year, and a Weekly Drop-In at the chapel lounge every week. There is a strong parish council in Thornborough and a regular magazine – the *Thornborough News* – which is free to all households in both the parishes, faithfully recording details of our activities and advertising events in the calendar to come.

Due to its size, Thornton is classified as a Parish Meeting and so does not have a Parish Council. The Parish Clerk and Parish Secretary, however, actively involve their community in a variety of local events. As you will have noticed many organisations also span both Thornborough and Thornton!

One interesting aspect of our two villages is how many names have survived decades and, in some cases, hundreds of years. For example, Thornton College has preserved the names of the previous Lords of Thornton Manor in their house system: Ingleton, Tyrell and Cavendish. Thornton was an established place of learning as far back as 1467, when a grammar school was founded. In Thornborough, names such as Baker, Bunce, Capel, Cranwell, Goodger and Howard have endured for centuries. We are used to seeing these and other familiar names in the visitors' book at St Mary's Church when people from far-off places briefly return to their birthplace or to that of their ancestors.

TWYFORD, CHARNDON & POUNDON

Twyford is a small village in the Aylesbury Vale district of Buckinghamshire. The parish includes the hamlets of Poundon and Charndon.

The name Twyford is derived from the old English for double ford and refers to the double ford by which the old road from Twyford to Cowley crosses two streams at Twyford Mill. Charndon is situated 2 miles south-east of Twyford. The name Charndon derives from old English and means 'Cærda's hill'. A Congregational chapel was built here in 1825, but is now long gone.

Poundon is situated just over a mile south-west of Twyford. Again Poundon is derived from old English, but it is uncertain exactly where the first part comes from, although the second comes from the word 'dun' meaning 'hill'. Poundon has a thriving public house, The Sow & Pigs, which is popular for food.

The Great Central railway (soon to be HS2) crosses the north-east corner of the parish and the Bletchley and Oxford section of the London and North Western railway (soon to be the East West link) had a station called Marsh Gibbon and Poundon within the parish (now a house). The River Ouse separates the village from Oxfordshire, to the west.

Rural and sparsely populated, the area is isolated as the roads to the village from the west and east serve only Twyford and the village core is on a spur which terminates near the parish church. The lack of passing traffic is a significant factor in the present tranquil character of Twyford.

The village retains a strong community spirit, with numerous village events. It has a Church of England parish church, URC chapel, C of E primary school, village hall, public house (The Crown) and recreation ground where the village cricket and football teams play. The village shop has recently been turned into a community shop run by a group of hardworking volunteers. Twyford has a resident artist and his work can be seen decorating the inside of the brick bus shelter, along with depictions of the village celebrating the Queen's Silver, Gold and Diamond Jubilees over the years in the village hall.

Twyford was mentioned in the Domesday Book in 1086 and was one of the fifty parishes in Oxfordshire and Buckinghamshire included within the boundaries of the Bernwood Forest in the 12th century. The village has shrunk significantly since the medieval period, but evidence

Twyford and Charndon

of inhabitancy can still be seen from the air in many of the surrounding fields.

The Church of England Parish Church of the Assumption of the Blessed Virgin Mary in the village of Twyford is 12th-century. Close

to the church is the vicarage, which incorporates part of a 15th-century house consisting of a hall, now divided into two floors, with its original roof and solar. In Church Street are several 17th-century houses and cottages, among which is the old Red Lion Inn. Twyford watermill is over half a mile north-west from the church and is close to the double ford. The village is associated with Flora Thompson, the author of *Lark Rise to Candleford*. Flora Thompson's uncle, Thomas Whiting, a shoemaker, was a tenant of one of the cottages at Chilton Place. Flora Thompson would have visited here and perhaps lodged with her uncle and aunt whilst working at the post office in Twyford 1895.

During the Second World War, Poundon was the site of stations 53b and 53c of the Special Operations Executive (SOE). Poundon House was requisitioned by Winston Churchill and used as a training facility for female agents to be parachuted into enemy territories. This led to the formation just outside the village of the Poundon Hill Wireless station used as a Foreign and Commonwealth Office (FCO)/MI6 signal intelligence station. It was used as a base for government diplomatic and secret service communications during the Cold War. Now the site is used as a business park.

With all the railway developments around the villages the future is unclear, but with the strong community spirit and feeling of togetherness hopefully Twyford, Charndon and Poundon will continue to thrive into the next millennium.

🍁 WADDESDON

If you mention Waddesdon to most people, the usual reaction is 'Oh yes, Waddesdon Manor' and while it is true that the presence of this now-National Trust property is important to the village past and present there is more than just that to Waddesdon. There has been a settlement at the foot of the aptly named Spring Hill, an important source of water, since the Stone and Bronze Ages. The name of Waddesdon is derived from the Saxon words, wode (wood) and don (hill).

The village's fortunes have fluctuated over the centuries, but during the 18th and early 19th centuries, Waddesdon had a bad reputation for hostility to travellers. There is even a legend that a Welsh horse dealer was murdered in one of the local inns, which earned the village its nickname of 'Black Waddesdon'. During the 19th century, the so-called Waddesdon Giant, William Stevens, lived here. He weighed 38 stone and died, unsurprisingly, at the age of 46 at the Marlborough Arms, where a window had to be taken out so his body could be removed.

We still perform the ancient tradition of Beating the Bounds during Rogationtide (April or May) every seven years. 'Bounders' mark the length of the parish boundary and spank young boys over the marks 'to impress the place upon them'.

The arrival on the scene of the Rothschild family, first with Baron Ferdinand, was a turning point for the village. He purchased a large estate in 1874 and proceeded to build a country mansion, in the French style, which provided much needed secure jobs for local people, and also rebuilt much of the housing, moving the village further towards Aylesbury, clearing most of the original dwellings from the area near the church.

The Baron and his successors proved to be benevolent employers and supporters of village life. Waddesdon became a thriving community with at one point over 60 businesses and shops, catering for most of the needs of those who live here.

In 1880, the Baron also held a large party for local children in the Manor grounds. Known as 'The Baron's Treat', this was held annually and eventually attracted crowds in their thousands! The National Trust has revived this tradition recently with great success.

During the war years, Waddesdon Manor was home to a nursery school from Croydon and Waddesdon residents opened their homes to evacuees from London. Mr and Mrs James de Rothschild arranged for the rescue of a group of Jewish refugee boys from war-torn Germany at this time. Aged 7-15, 'The Cedars Boys' lived in a large house, The Cedars, in the village together with a Dr and Mrs Steinhart to care for them. Over 30 in all, the boys integrated into the local area, attending school, learning English and playing football. Most of them emigrated to the USA and two lads who started their football career in Waddesdon eventually played for the USA against England. They erected a plaque in the grounds of the Manor as a thank-you to the Rothschilds who had undoubtedly saved their lives.

Waddesdon had several attempts at providing schooling during the 18th and 19th centuries, but the first National School (run by the church) was opened in 1845 with provision for 150 pupils. More places were needed and a British (secular) school soon followed. The village continued to have two schools until they were amalgamated as Waddesdon

Village Primary. In 1962, a new secondary school was built on a site donated by Mrs Dorothy de Rothschild, and both schools now enjoy this pleasant location. The secondary school is a source of much pride for the village, having an enviable reputation across the county and a popular community library.

In 2018, we acquired a new Greenway path for walkers and cyclists from the Aylesbury Vale Parkway Station to Waddesdon Manor car park.

Waddesdon is still thriving, with a local shop and post office at the heart of our community. Clubs and classes are available in the Village Hall, the Methodist Hall, the Bowls Club, the Secondary School and the Football Pavilion – there is something for everyone.

🍁 WENDOVER

Wendover is a small market town at the foot of the Chiltern Hills on the edge of the Vale of Aylesbury. A thriving community with much to offer all ages, it is surrounded by woodland, farms and countryside yet is only fifty minutes away from London by train.

Over the centuries, the village, as Wendover is fondly called, has been owned by many famous people. Catherine of Aragon was granted Wendover twice; once when she married Arthur and then when she married Henry VIII! Henry then gave it to various of his wives. Today, Anne Boleyn Cottages and other names are redolent of the past.

The original settlement was centred near the church but over the years the pragmatic people of Wendover moved their businesses and homes as need changed. A 1965 book shows there were 13 grocers in the village – but now there is one excellent supermarket which knows and caters for its customers, as well as sourcing produce locally where it can. Current concerns include the implications of the closure of RAF Halton in 2022; it has been an integral part of the village since 1913, and also the impact that HS2 might have.

The village is largely self-sufficient with education across the school age range. One school's swimming pool is available for community use and gyms and other fitness initiatives abound, including splendid facilities at RAF Halton. Wendover Youth Centre provides many activities for teenagers, and for older villagers there is a wide variety of organisations and interest groups.

Wendover Woods are beautiful in the Spring when the bluebells flower but all year round there are activities for families to enjoy. Coombe Hill has spectacular views across the Vale attracting tourists to the village, and there is a hotel plus a range of restaurants, coffee shops and bars for all to enjoy.

Wendover never ceases to be friendly – and opens its wide arms to newcomers. On the formal side, we are officially a Dementia Friendly village and the Health Centre has a Friends group that provides transport to and from healthcare appointments. The Community Library runs well and The Lionel Abel Trust, created by the Lord of the Manor, supports Wendover by providing grants to its people and organisations.

Rope Walk Meadow now proudly houses the commemorative Community Orchard. A fruit tree has been planted for each man killed in World War One and named on the War Memorial. In future these trees, like silent soldiers, will yield fruit for anyone to pick and provide shade to sit under.

Wendover remembers its past but plans for future generations. It also keeps certain traditions. A charter for a twice-yearly fair was first granted in 1214. In 1464/5, this charter added a Thursday market which is still excellent today. In recent years the carnival has been revived and every other year 'Wendover Celebrates...'. Last but not least, there is the annual movement of sheep through the village. This has been happening for countless generations and continues today to the delight of villagers and the irritation of car drivers!

Whatever happens to the RAF site or with HS2 one thing is sure: Wendover people will always welcome you and the sheep will move freely.

🍁 WHADDON

Whaddon is a small village with more history than houses. The village was first referred to in the *Anglo-Saxon Chronicle* (written in the 9th century) as Hwætædun, which means 'wheat hill'. On the edge of Aylesbury Vale, we are in the ever-growing shadow of Milton Keynes but are distinctly separate from it. A lot of ancient Anglo-Saxon farmland has been swallowed by the growing city, but in return we have easy access to a ten-screen cinema, indoor skydiving, indoor skiing, and several miles of shops. However, there is no bus service

– so reaching these amenities depends upon a car, a six-mile walk or a taxi.

The last Saxon to hold the Manor of Whaddon was Edward Cilt, a member of the Court of Edward the Confessor. Under the Normans, it became the Gift of the King and Whaddon Hall was rebuilt. Hunting brought many kings to Whaddon and Henry III named us Whaddon Chase, to which Henry VIII later added the title 'Royal'. We still have the remains of the Sober Oak where Henry began his day's hunt, finishing it four miles away with a huge picnic under another tree, known, for obvious reasons, as the Drunken Elm. There is another historic oak tree in the grounds of Whaddon Hall. Earl Grey de Wilton inherited the Hall in 1562 and employed as his secretary a certain Edmund Spenser. Since Lord Grey lived in the Hall, it is certain that part of Spenser's epic poem *The Faerie Queene* was written here.

Of the many owners of Whaddon Hall, the most colourful has to be Browne Willis. A fine antiquarian, it is a pity that his handwriting was illegible. He did much entertaining but dressed like a pauper. Wearing two or three coats tied up by an old leather belt with an ancient cloak on top, he was described by one lady as 'very unpleasant to sit next to at dinner'. But he restored many local churches and built a chapel in Fenny Stratford, from which the famous Fenny Poppers, six small cast iron mugs stuffed with gunpowder, are fired each year on St Martin's Day. Browne Willis himself started the tradition and the annual Fenny Popper Festival in August has become a memorial to him.

In the village itself, we have the 16th-century Lowndes Arms pub, home to gin festivals, BBQ evenings and a popular weekly quiz night. St Mary's Church replaced the timber Saxon church during the 11th century, and proudly displays a list of its vicars going back to 1103. The church is complemented by the 'new' Chapel, opened in 1907, and both are still well attended.

For years, the Weatherby family (of horse racing fame) opened their grounds for the Church Fete – there is nothing like the sound of a brass band playing in the herbaceous borders as you drink Pimm's on a sunny June afternoon! The Weatherby family still own many acres round here, and there are fond memories of both Alison Weatherby, President of the Whaddon WI for many years, and Major Christopher Weatherby who sang in the church choir, and tapped his foot loudly against the pew if the sermon went on for too long!

The Recreation Ground has been newly refurbished, and Whaddon's younger children have a wonderful football pitch, swings, slide and climbing frames to use when not attending our very own village school. This is a Church of England First School, with approximately 50 children who benefit from small class sizes and a caring environment with strong community links. The school is central to village life in many ways, and the whole main street shuts for the May Fayre parade, where the 'King' and 'Queen' lead the procession in a sports car, followed by every child in the school in fancy dress, and then slow-driving floats from various village associations, with cheering crowds lining the street. Whaddon children have been dancing round the maypole for centuries and organising this annual tradition has been the school's responsibility for the last 200 years.

The focal point of the village is Jubilee Hall, built in 1935 for the Silver Jubilee of King George V and Queen Mary. It held the first meeting of the Whaddon WI in 1936 and now hosts village events from harvest suppers and discos to yoga class and the annual Whaddon Show by the ingenious, talented and ever resourceful Whaddon Entertainers.

A proud plaque in Jubilee Hall celebrates the fact that MI6 Communications used Whaddon as an outpost of Bletchley Park during the Second World War. In 2016, the last-living former covert agent in France had a video-link with our villagers in Jubilee Hall, celebrating this unique history.

The Second World War brought Whaddon's finest hour. Though everyone knows of the work done at Bletchley Park, the vital work done at Whaddon and Hanslope was top secret for many years. The Hall was taken over as the headquarters of MI6 Communications Section VIII with the vital task of spreading information gathered at Bletchley to embassies, military commanders and agents abroad in total secrecy. This was done via two powerful transmitters installed on Windy Ridge (whose groundwork is still visible in the field next to the church). The Ridge was heavily guarded so the locals had no idea what was going on.

The stable block in the Hall was used by 300 specialists to develop new spy equipment, such as Ascension which enabled aircraft to communicate with the ground without the risk of signals being picked up by German radio beacons. Before Q created gadgets for James Bond, specialists at Whaddon Hall were inventing covert equipment such as an agent's MkVII attaché case with built-in wireless set – for which villagers supplied old suitcases!

Today, only one or two ladies can demonstrate knowledge of the traditional Bucks Point lacemaking that used to be the bread-and-butter of almost every woman and child in the village prior to the introduction of machine-made lace in the 1820s. Instead, our 21st-century pursuits include a village Facebook community that posts on anything from stray lambs and local band gigs to charity collections, a monthly village Book Club, and meetings of the two WI's, Whaddon WI and Whaddon Night Owlers WI, that our village supports.

🍁 WHELPLEY HILL

Whelpley Hill is a small but friendly village set in beautiful countryside on the border with Hertfordshire, between Chesham, Bovingdon, Berkhamsted and its neighbouring parish village, Ashley Green.

The village was known as Wolf Hill during the Middle Ages and it is steeped with history. There is evidence of an Iron Age hillfort and both the Royal Air Force and the USAAF used the local Berry Farm during the Second World War.

In 1986, local farmer Tony Harman immortalised Whelpley Hill in his best-selling book *Seventy Summers*. Highlighting the charms of village life, the book became a hit BBC series written and narrated by him.

Sadly, there is no church in Whelpley Hill now. Both the Baptist Chapel, closed in 1948, and the Anglican Church, sold around 2006, are now private homes. However, services are held occasionally in the Village Hall.

Whelpley Hill Village Hall, also known as Coronation Hall, was originally built in the 1920s on land given to the village by a local farmer. Following a community-funded refurbishment in 2010, the hall is now used by various organisations and clubs for ballet classes, fitness and theatre groups, children's parties and of course, meetings of the WI.

The White Hart is a lovely old village pub set in the idyllic surrounding countryside. Open seven days a week, they offer locally sourced meat and help raise a lot of money for local charities.

At the village centre is Whelpley Hill Park where there are over 80 park homes. First established in the late 1960s, the homes are built on 'pan handles' – hard aircraft stands on the former airfield used during the Second World War. Elderly villagers recall seeing Flying Fortress bombers crossing the village lane from Berry Farm to be parked on these pan handles in wartime. It is now a popular and attractive park home site.

There is an abundance of wildlife in this rural area – muntjac deer often find their way into gardens, as well as badgers, foxes, rabbits, little owls, barn owls, red kites and bats. And the notorious glis glis dormouse, found only in the Chiltern area, often finds its way into people's lofts and creates havoc!

The Chiltern Heritage trail passes through the centre of the village – this is a 50-mile circular route that passes through all 14 parishes in the Chiltern District – visiting beautiful scenery, picturesque villages and heritage sites, all of which are embodied in Whelpley Hill.

🍁 WING

Wing occupies an extraordinary position both geographically and historically; there has been a settlement here since the Iron Age and the Church of All Saints is one of the oldest Saxon churches in the country. The village is mentioned in the Domesday book, and recent excavations in the grounds of the old church school revealed burial sites dating back to the first millennium AD.

Geographically, Wing enjoys an elevated position on a sandstone ridge at the edge of Buckinghamshire, close to the boundary with Bedfordshire. The stream that runs around the hill flows into the Great Ouse and on to the Wash, but the watershed with the Thames basin is less than a mile away.

Nowadays, the noise of the traffic mingles with the cry of the jackdaws round the church tower, along with the red kites and the buzzards. When the wind is in the east we hear the trains on the Euston line and the aircraft turning towards Luton airport.

The village has had its share of threats and upheavals in the past; during the 1970s this area was chosen as a possible site for London's third airport, many of the surrounding villages would have been lost and Wing would have been sitting on the perimeter fence!

Today, Wing is a village where very few leave and where there is a real sense of belonging and worth. We have families going back generations. Why do we all stay? For a start we have so many more amenities than most villages, along with regular buses, two doctors' surgeries, a well-stocked shop, a post office, chemist, hairdressers and library, not forgetting two pubs and two restaurants, plus of course the fish and chip shop. We have a main line station ten minutes' drive away that can get you to London in just over half an hour. If you want bigger shops then Leighton Buzzard and Milton Keynes are close by, so everything is catered for.

We are a friendly village with a sense of community at its heart. There are so many clubs and sporting activities for children and adults, young and old, we are spoilt for choice. On our recreation ground there are tennis courts, a bowling green and football pitches. We have a lovely village green free of traffic and ideal for young children to have fun playing safely on the swings and slides. To keep the more elderly on their toes, there is a luncheon club and day centre run by volunteers. With so much to do it is easy to meet new people, make friends and share experiences.

For quieter moments away from the excitement of busy village life, there is a National Trust property, Ascott House, with beautiful grounds to roam in or just take the many footpaths that abound. A local spinney, maintained by enthusiastic volunteers, provides the perfect retreat for any walker looking for a moment's solitude. But you're never alone for long: a walk in Wing can take a long time as everyone stops to chat, especially if you have a dog!

Many of our clubs and societies meet in our Village Hall. As well as a large well-equipped hall with a stage, suitable for shows and receptions, it houses smaller meeting rooms, our community library, an opportunity shop and a large kitchen.

🍁 WINGRAVE

Wingrave is a village halfway between Aylesbury and Wing, just off the A418. Overlooking the Vale of Aylesbury, this ancient hilltop settlement appears in the Domesday Book as Withungrave. This comes from the Old English 'Wiwinga graf' or 'Weoinga graf' meaning 'the grove of the people referred to by Wing' or 'the grove of the people of the heathen temple'!

Today the village is home to approximately 1,500 people from all walks of life. Past famous inhabitants include Ian Dury (of the Blockheads), Peter Cook, Michael Portillo, George Griffin and Bill Drummond, who famously burned £1m. Current residents include actors, dancers, choreographers and the body double for the actor Chris Hemsworth!

Over the years, villagers have benefited from the bequests of prosperous residents such as Thomas Pratt, Elizabeth Theed and Sir Richard Goddard. Pratts Charity is still in existence today, more than 400 years after Thomas Pratt signed his will on 17 November 1614.

Perhaps the person to have most influence on the village is Hannah de Rothschild, the only child of Mayer Amschel Rothschild. Born in 1851, Hannah's family moved to nearby Mentmore when she was just four years old. They owned a grand country estate that became known as Mentmore Towers and Hannah inherited this from her father when he died in 1874. The Estate comprised £2m, Mentmore Towers and its contents, and 4,500 acres. This made Hannah one of the wealthiest women in England.

Although Hannah did not live in the village, she became one of its main benefactors. She purchased land and property, demolishing derelict and dilapidated buildings. In their place she built 35 houses with the distinct 'Rothschild finish' of white rendered walls and black timber, bearing Hannah's monogram. Hannah let these cottages to villagers at low rents. Over the years she also established and fully funded the village Infant School, a Reading Room for adults, a Recreation Ground for sports and a children's playground.

When Hannah married Archibald Primrose, the 5th Earl of Rosebery, it was the wedding of the year. She was given away by the Prime Minister, Benjamin Disraeli, and Edward, Prince of Wales signed the register. In Wingrave, the church bells rang to proclaim that Miss Hannah had become the Countess of Rosebery. The children of the village all wore outfits provided by Hannah. A public tea was held in the school and this was followed by a concert which opened with 'And now the Nuptial Knot is Tied', a new composition by George Griffin. Lord Rosebery later became Foreign Secretary but, sadly, Hannah died of typhoid fever in 1890, four years before he became Prime Minister. After her death, Hannah's influence continued to be reflected in the way in which the Mentmore Estate was run and the villagers of Wingrave continued to benefit from the generosity of the Roseberys.

Hannah's legacy to Wingrave includes one of its important buildings: the Old Manor House (now known as Mount Tabor), built in 1878. This was leased to William Russell Stewart Freeman, wealthy proprietor of Aldridge's Horse Repository of St Martins Lane, London. Mr Freeman purchased the house and lands in 1898 for £17,300. He seemed to enjoy the role of Squire giving his time and money and participating socially in the village. In 1905 there was a great scandal in the county when Mary Eveline, Freeman's eldest daughter, eloped with Algernon de Vere Capell, the 8th Earl of Essex (complete with ladder at the bedroom window!). Mary Eveline and Algernon divorced in 1926 after which she continued to live in the Manor House for many years. On the outbreak of the Second World War, the house was leased to the Czech Government, exiled in England under their leader Dr Eduard Benes. The Czechs remained at the house until 1945. By way of thanks they provided the bus shelter that still stands at Wingrave crossroads on the A418. The links have continued over the years with visits from Václav Havel (last President of Czechoslovakia 1989-1992 and first President of the Czech Republic 1993-2003) and the Czech and Slovak Ambassadors. In 1972, the house was acquired by the MacIntyre Schools of Westoning. A purpose-built school for children with extreme special needs is now on the site and the Manor House has been converted into private dwellings.

Another building of note is St Peter and St Paul's Church which stands at the highest point in the village and dates back to 1190. In 1786, a villager called Elizabeth Theed lost her way in the local fields during a storm, but was able to find her way back home by following the sound of the church bells. In gratitude, she left a piece of land to the church so that every year on Feast Day, the aisles could be strewn with rushes. That tradition continues to this day.

Wingrave today is a thriving community with something for everyone. Clubs on offer cover hobbies from reading and art to rambling. There are two choirs, bingo, a youth club, Brownies, the Wingrave Players, the Heritage Association. We come together at the Rose and Crown, over a summer barbecue or Winter Family Friday at the Community Centre. And, of course, there's the WI, playing an active role since 1923.

🍁 WINSLOW

Winslow is a small rural market town midway along the A413 between Aylesbury and Buckingham.

In 792, King Offa of Mercia gave the estate of Winslow to his newly founded Abbey of St Albans. The population stood at just 100 in the Domesday Book of 1087. But today, that number is closer to 6,000.

And Winslow wears its history well – its ancient buildings are clearly visible and are all included in local community life.

Winslow Hall, designed by Sir Christopher Wren, hosts an open-air opera every summer in its grounds. The popular August Bank Holiday Show and the annual Hunt on Boxing Day are in the Home Field opposite.

St Laurence Church is used by two faiths and its faded murals survey the congregation as they have for 800 years. The church is lucky to have a strong four-part choir with both adults and children singing a wide range of services. Keach's Meeting Place, where dissenting Baptists sang hymns to the disapproval of their officers, is cared for and open for view. But as there is no electricity here, a daytime viewing is recommended!

The Christmas Fat Stock Show, which was always held in the Cattle Market, has now been reinstated in the Market Square. Local farmers attend bringing their prize cattle and sheep to be judged and then auctioned off. The Square is straw-lined and many people from Winslow and neighbouring villages come to watch the auctioneer conduct his business.

We take pride in once winning recognition in the Best Bucks town challenge. New houses, a new secondary school and a new special needs school all nestle among trees to keep our rural roots – and it's pleasing to see the allotments are still tended with great care. A recently planted arboretum offers another spot to sit and watch bowls matches. The park features outdoor gym equipment, swings, slides and roundabouts for the children, and croquet is played as well as football and cricket.

An army of volunteers runs the local library and the Big Society is much in existence organising activities such as afternoon teas, singing for pleasure, games and card groups. Volunteer car drivers bring people less able to get about to these gatherings, but also to appointments with the doctor or dentist.

There is a good, reliable bus service these days to Aylesbury and Milton Keynes. One member recalls a Red Rover bus arriving in the town on Sundays to take passengers to Aylesbury to the cinema but you were lucky if you could get a seat. Steam trains once ran to Oxford and Bletchley and the station was bedecked with flowerbeds. Now, if plans go ahead, trains will once again stop at Winslow.

The Winslow Players drama group, formed over 50 years ago, put on three productions a year, with plays in spring and autumn and a pantomime at Christmas. There are also various societies and clubs and a morning and evening WI for those wishing to take part.

Shops range from a hardware store, several hairdressers, nail and beauty salons, florists, butchers and supermarkets. The Lions and Rotary Clubs also play a big part in the town's social calendar with charitable events such as the Bonfire and Firework display, Carols in the Market Square and the Father Christmas float which travels around the town.

Winslow is a truly caring community where the old mix with the new and it's a rare day that you can walk down the street without bumping into a friend to catch up with.